POETRY DAILY

ESSENTIALS

2007

edited by

Diane Boller and Don Selby

SOURCEBO
NAPERVILL

D1167003

Sourcebooks and the colophon are registered trademarks of
Sourcebooks, Inc.

Published by Sourcebooks, Inc.
P.O. Box 4410, Naperville, Illinois 60567-4410
(630) 961-3900
Fax: (630) 961-2168
www.sourcebooks.com

Library of Congress Cataloging-in-Publication Data

Poetry Daily Essentials 2007 / [compiled by] Don Selby and Diane Boller.
    p. cm.
 Includes index.
 ISBN-13: 978-1-4022-0927-7
 ISBN-10: 1-4022-0927-4
 1. American poetry—21st century. I. Selby, Don. II. Boller, Diane. III.
Title: Poetry Daily Essentials 2007

PS617.A18 2007
811'.608—dc22

2006036878

Printed and bound in the United States of America.
    VP 10 9 8 7 6 5 4 3 2 1

About the Editors

Don Selby co-founded *Poetry Daily* with Diane Boller and Rob Anderson following a twenty-year career in the law publishing industry. He is a graduate of Swarthmore College and the University of Virginia School of Law. He lives in Charlottesville, Virginia.

In addition to her work with *Poetry Daily*, **Diane Boller** has pursued careers in law and publishing. She is a graduate of the University of Virginia, and the George Mason University School of Law. She lives in Charlottesville, Virginia.

Order of Poems

About the Editors iii

Acknowledgments ix

Introduction xi

My Father's Track and Field Medal | Edward Hirsch | 2
Schemes | Alison Brackenbury | 3
The Evening Star | Louise Glück | 4
Edge | Eamon Grennan | 5
Riffing Deciduous | Brendan Galvin | 6
Sunflowers in a Field | Daniel Anderson | 7
Winter Field | Joanna Klink | 9
Death of a Gull | Cleopatra Mathis | 10
Huge Fragility | Tony Dent | 12
Hummingbird | Dorianne Laux | 13
Sand | Patty Seyburn | 14
Late Beauty | Karl Kirchwey | 15
Honey Suckles | Daniel Wolff | 18
Home Front and Gardens | Elton Glaser | 19
Twilight: After Haying | Jane Kenyon | 20
Virgil: *from the* Second Georgic | Virgil | 21
Concerning a Young Woman | Sappho | 25
The Spanish Lover | Claudia Emerson | 26
Oasis | Dana Goodyear | 27
First Love | Wisława Szymborska | 28
Latents | Kay Ryan | 29
Lesser Evils | Joel Brouwer | 30
Marvell Noir | Ann Lauinger | 31
Travel Plans | Leslie Monsiur | 32
Animal Self | Randy Blasing | 33
Medical Advice | Joel Sheerin | 34
Sounding Aboard the *Rafaella* | Rex Wilder | 35
The Welcome | David Joel Friedman | 36
Re-Gifting | Vona Groarke | 37
Oatmeal | Peggy Shumaker | 38
13 Haiku About My Husband and Current State of Happiness | Mary Kane | 39
Anent the Yellow Field, Fa-La | Brooks Haxton | 41
A Marriage Must Be Worked At | Michael Chitwood | 42
Anatomy of Failure | Meghan O'Rourke | 43

And Day Brought Back My Night	Geoffrey Brock	45
The Long Marriage	Jeffrey Skinner	45
Takeoff	Alan Shapiro	46
The Hoopoe's Crown	Jacqueline Osherow	47
Acrostic: Outhouse	Paula Bohince	53
First Breath Last Breath	Antler	54
At Home	Hugo Claus	55
A Lamb by Its Ma	Chase Twichell	56
Horseneck Beach Odalisque	William Logan	57
Absence	Anne Marie Macari	58
Obedience, Or the Lying Tale	Jennifer Chang	60
My Mother's Hands	David Woo	62
Near Hag's Head	Daniel Tobin	63
Peter Street	Peter Sirr	64
The United States	Rodney Jones	65
The Demise of Camembert	Ron Slate	67
Elena Ceaucescu's Bed	W.D. Snodgrass	69
A Stick, A Cup, A Bowl, A Comb	Darta Wier	70
Board Book & the Costume of a Whooping Crane	David Wojahn	72
Blackbird	C.K. Wiliams	75
Contract Law	Michael Scharf	77
About Money	Liam Rector	78
You Miss It	Max Garland	80
The Pier Aspiring	Thomas Lux	82
Suddenly	Louis Simpson	83
Nothing's As It Should Be	Robert Phillips	84
On Broadway	Timothy Liu	85
When the Watchman Saw the Light	C.P. Cavafy	87
Our Generation	Carl Dennis	88
[I want to build]	Friedrich Holderlin	90
Hephaistos	Liam Aungier	91
Icarus Descending	Carol Edelstein	92
Noah at Dusk	Terri Witek	93
The Shout	Simon Armitage	94
The Population	Peter Campion	95
The View From Zero Bridge	Lynn Aarti Chandhok	96
Subway Seethe	J. Allyn Rosser	97
Selling Out	Dennis O'Driscoll	98
Chess Match Ends in Fight	David Hernandez	99
Kitty Oppenheimer Tends Louis Slotin after an Accident in the Lab	John Canaday	100

The Bear	Dan Chiasson	101
Who the Meek Are Not	Mary Karr	102
The Private Meditations of John Wyclif: On Angels	Thom Satterlee	103
Far Niente	Heather McHugh	104
Elegance	Linda Gregg	105
Description of a Lost Thing	Charles Simic	106
They Had Torn Off My Face at the Office	Ted Kooser	107
Empty Similes	Bob Hicok	108
My First Mermaid	Debora Greger	109
Two Children Threatened by a Nightingale	Eric Pankey	111
Two Wheeler Spins	Colette Inez	112
The Fire Museum	Jennifer Fumiko Cahill	113
House Guest	Alexandra Teague	114
Ghazal	Marilyn Hacker	115
Enemies of Enormity	David Rivard	116
I Followed a Ribbon	Jesse Ball	118
Resistance	Peter Leight	119
Miss Congeniality	Laura Kasischke	121
Pain Tries to Think of Something	Laurie Lamon	123
Dress Rehearsal	Floyd Skloot	124
Six at the Beginning	Deborah Bogen	125
talking at blerancourt	David Antin	126
Small parts slowly	Mary Molinary	136
Faced with 8:38	Mary Molinary	136
On us too	Mary Molinary	137
Very Hot Day	Michael Ryan	139
To Failure	Tim Skeen	140
Trying to Be Penitent	J.T. Barbarese	141
Stroke	William Greenway	143
Racial Profile #2	June Jordan	144
Sursum Corda	Hillel Schwartz	146
The Chair She Sits In	Alberto Ríos	149
Blue Umbrella	Gail Mazur	150
Report from My Own Backyard	Paula Closson Buck	152
Used One Speed, Princeton	Daisy Fried	154
One-Time Use	Richard D. Allen	155
Feeding the Fire	Edison Jennings	156
Aristophanes at the Woodpile	Robert Chute	157
Snow	Kevin Hart	158
Mycorrhizae	Talvikki Ansel	159

Army Tales	Kevin Prufer	160
New Year, with Nipperkin	Richard Kenney	162
Sylvia	Gerald Stern	163
Charles Street, Late November	Erica Funkhouser	164
Keepsake	Philip White	165
Wishful Rhetoric	Kevin Stein	166
"Off in the darkness hourses moved restlessly"	Albert Goldbarth	167
The Unlasting	John Koethe	168
Darkness Starts	Christian Wiman	178
Tree Ghost	Yusef Komunyakaa	179
Death, Etc.	Maxine Kumin	180
Appalachian Farewell	Charles Wright	182
Prescience	Franz Wright	183
Big Doors	Richard Tillinghast	184
To You	Kevin A. González	185
To the Soul	W.S. Merwin	186
White Heron Pond	David Baker	187
The Insistence of Beauty	Stephen Dunn	189
Ars Poetica	Czesław Miłosz	191
Testament	Gustaf Sobin	193
My Mother's Poem	David Wagoner	194
The Pity of Punctuation	Susan Hahn	195
The Locust Song	Albert Goldbarth	197
In a Field	Elizabeth Spires	199
Rattlesnakes Hammered on the Wall	Ray Gonzalez	201
Logo Rhythms	Karl Elder	202
Lullabye	Amanda Jernigan	206
Old Age	Daniel Hoffman	207
Postmortem	Clare Rossini	208
Still Life With Jonquils	Andrea Hollander Budy	209
Miscegenation	Natasha Trethewey	210
Up Late, Reading Whitman	James Kimbrell	211
You Got a Song, Man	Martín Espada	215
Jittery	Jim Simmerman	217
Counterman	Paul Violi	219
International Incidents	Robert Hershon	221
Some Days I Feel Like Janet Leigh	Barbara Hamby	222
Local Heroes	Thomas Lynch	223
Black Labrador	David Young	225

Acknowledgments

Poetry Daily would not be 10 years old without the personal loyalty and generous financial contributions of readers, poets, editors, publishers, and sponsors. To stand for these stalwart friends, we here acknowledge the extraordinary support of Lannan Foundation, the National Endowment for the Arts, and the Virginia Commission for the Arts, from whose tireless work on behalf of the literary arts we have taken inspiration all these years, as well as Jim Gibson, Carole Weinstein, Laura Horn, and Tree Swenson, whose constant gifts of professional example, wise counsel, and warm friendship hearten us *daily*. With these, we want to take this and every opportunity to thank *all* who have joined with us in our mission to make the best in contemporary poetry easily available to everyone, everywhere.

Introduction

On April 7, 2007, *Poetry Daily* (www.poems.com) marks its <u>tenth anniversary</u> online! In celebration, we are delighted to present *Poetry Daily Essentials 2007*, a selection of poems featured on our web site since we assembled our first anthology, published by Sourcebooks in 2003.

Every day of every year, *Poetry Daily* presents a new poem (and sometimes two or three…) from the best new books and journals in English, from publishers large and small. For thousands of readers around the world who have made *Poetry Daily* their personal home page, our daily poem is literally the first thing they read each day. If you are one of these readers, *Poetry Daily Essentials 2007* is a compact reminder of past pleasures you can carry with you through your *offline* day. If you've not yet visited us online, this selection will give you a taste of the wide range and sources of great poems to be found on *Poetry Daily* from day to day, week to week, year to year (and *decade to decade!*).

We've done our best to represent the variety and depth of the poetry that appears on *Poetry Daily*, so enjoy *Poetry Daily Essentials 2007* and then drop in online! You will be joining readers from all walks of life – poets and teachers and students, to be sure – but also the many quiet thousands who carry on their devotion to contemporary poetry in offices and on work sites, in community centers and libraries, in retirement homes and military bases – and, no kidding, "all the ships at sea": one of our earliest correspondents wrote to us from a research ship in Antarctica!

As you will know, *Poetry Daily* did not create the audience for authentic poetry that has always existed in every era. But our constant pleasure, all these years, has been to help that audience to grow and to enjoy a broader and richer experience of contemporary poetry by providing access to exciting new poetry from even the most obscure journal and chapbook publisher – to do all we can to serve as matchmaker between poet and reader. Everything we do, from our daily online selections and the many other special editorial features and news links found on our site, to this new anthology, is done to help readers follow the poems that inspire them to the books and journals where a still richer experience of their favorite poets' work will be found.

So, once again, welcome to *Poetry Daily* *off*line, and when you've had a chance to enjoy this special collection, look for more poetry and special features at www.poems.com. We'll be there for you every day!

Diane Boller
Don Selby
Editors

POETRY DAILY

DAILY

ESSENTIALS

2007

My Father's Track and Field Medal, 1932

Cup the tarnished metal in your palm.
Look closely and you'll see a squirrel
scampering up a beech-wood in the forest.
You'll see a cardinal flaming in the branches.
You'll see a fleet-footed antelope racing
through the woods ahead of the hunters.

Edward Hirsch
Five Points
Volume 9, Number 2

Schemes

Who plants forsythia now? It is not tasteful;
Too ragged, tall, and dull when leaves are out.
But see the sparrows rush into its heart,
Eyes stroke it, raw and golden as a shout.

Alison Brackenbury
Poetry Wales
Volume 41, Number 3
Autumn 2005

The Evening Star

Tonight, for the first time in many years,
there appeared to me again
a vision of the earth's splendor:

in the evening sky
the first star seemed
to increase in brilliance
as the earth darkened

until at last it could grow no darker.
And the light, which was the light of death,
seemed to restore to earth

its power to console. There were
no other stars. Only the one
whose name I knew

as in my other life I did her
injury: Venus,
star of the early evening,

to you I dedicate
my vision, since on this blank surface

you have cast enough light
to make my thought
visible again.

Louise Glück
Averno
Farrar, Straus and Giroux

Edge

When I'd walked out to the sea surfing and spuming
into meerschaum heaps of lettuce-tinted gauze –
breakers becoming light then noise, the ocean raging
and rearranging this long spit of sand like a life
at the mercy of circumstance – I saw the north wind

drive trillions of sandgrains to scour every last trace
of what the previous tide had done, and gulls snatch
huge clamshells from the swirl and smash them
to get at and gobble each salt, soft-bodied helplessness
at the heart of its own broken home, and I felt caught

between water-violence and the gulls' patience,
between shifting ground I stood on and the thunder-
turbulence of water, between a slowly disappearing
ceiling of cloud and the blue sky-cupola it leaves
behind, between titanic ocean-roar and the ticking heart.

Eamon Grennan
AGNI 62

Riffing Deciduous

Summer, old bore, though we love the ways
  you reduce everything to five shades
    of green, one of these days

in a fall of soft tonnage, your stranglehold
  on the obvious must end. We need those
    deciduous farewells that reveal

from cranberry bog to hogsback,
  from seagrass to sky at dusk, not red
    but its modulations: solferino, murrey,

minium, not yellow but vitelline and those
  others nameless as the obscurer insects.
    On one of those clarified mornings,

in a nest like a straw handbag
  hung to the weather, in a fright wig out on a limb,
    in cones of grass and false beards

precariously woven, the instinctive faith
  of birds will reveal itself to a walker's eye.
    As if to prove all things must have their time,

the textures of fox sparrows will be
  no longer subtle, but flashy and necessary,
    until we can trust that if we pay attention

we'll hear the groaning into being
  of things believed in though unseen – a gasp
    as chives gain the air, and even before equinox

the sound of a rubbed balloon
  as wings chafe cold from the winter-brittle blue.

Brendan Galvin
Habitat: New and Selected Poems, 1965-2005
Louisiana State University Press

Sunflowers in a Field

Sunflowers in a field.
Goldfinches everywhere.
They gorge on seed. They rise
To rest along the power line, then fall
Like drizzled lemon drops, like lozenges
Of candied yellow light.
Two weeks a year, goldfinches
Gather on sunflowers here.
These evenings after supper,
You see them in the honey-soft glow
As if they'd trapped and somehow stored
The rapture of September's sun.
You see goldfinches flicker
Among sunflower lanes,
Through mortal tides of light,
Through streams of apricot and chardonnay,
And you resolve to live
Your life with greater sympathy.
Sunflowers bowing their char black dials,
Their petals twist and writhe
Like fires, like silk coronas blazing west.
How inconceivable, then,
The pewter cold-front clouds,
The shabby settlement of crow and wren.
Though no one hears the oath,
You shall, you tell yourself,
Forgo deceit, increase the tithe.
Atone. Forgive. Embrace. You watch
Goldfinches and sunflowers both
Begin to fade. By subtle green degrees
They shed that bullion luster of the sun
Until the finches ricochet
Like flints among the drowsing flower heads.
Perhaps, as I have done,
You'll pace the darkling half mile home,
Intent on picking up the telephone
To reconcile with long-lost friends.
You will apologize, concede.

You'll vow to never, ever, ever let
Such distance grow again.
But then you reach your door and find
The day diminished to a thin blue rind
Of light above the township silhouette.
How nice a hot bath sounds.
Dessert. An herbal tea.
Perhaps you'll read the Arts
And Leisure pages of *The Daily News*.
With every stair you climb
Sleep settles just a little more behind
The knees, beneath the shoulder blades.
The calls, you tell yourself,
Perhaps some other time.

Daniel Anderson
The Southern Review
Spring 2005

Winter Field

What better witness than this evening snow,
its steady blind quiet, its eventual
completeness, a talc smoothing every surface

through the lumen tricks of ice.
No one who comes here hastens to leave,
though the mineral winter makes a dull

math of cold inside the bones, a numbness
thinning into each fingertip and eye.
Faint injury traveling toward earth

in shifting silence, a softness in the weather
passing through us, dark moods of snows –
a sense of peace so deep we extend out

into the blackness of our lives, dread and failure,
and feel no hint of terror, only the premonition
of drift-design, the stars behind the snow

burning in ancient immanence over the field.
What lights a world gone blank with despair?
You were here once; you will be here again.

Joanna Klink
Boston Review
January/February 2006

Death of a Gull

Worse than his pain was his acceptance,
the wing loosely dragging beside him
while he did his best not to notice. As if the impossibility
might drop away, he ambled, a hen's shuffle
from oceanside toward the plovers' nesting ground,
but the little birds came diving, driving him back.
Beak open, he hissed like a swan, his only show.
Another gull glided down, just one – perhaps his mate –
companions side by side until he ignored
the cues for flight. She spiraled out of the path
of passersby, but he only turned his head away,
like a toddler's shy aside, to make the intruder disappear.

Day and night turned over, the waves
close then far. The weight dangling at his side
grew heavier and he learned to fix his eye
on the middle distance. Alone and offered up,
he roosted there, suffering the tide-rich sand
and the roving metal-throated birds
from which he once stole fish. The spewing waves,
the crabs awash, haphazard heads and claws,
offered nothing he wanted to eat.
The whole thing reeked. Overhead, the hypnotic
sequined blue glittered and teased.

The green sea went about its business,
sifting, hooking, grinding. Bottom waters
boiled and rose, feeding all the frenzied
multiplying cells, which brought the little fish,
the bigger fish, and then the seal,
whose lackadaisical tossing off of bones
made him the birds' life of the party.
The crippled gull heard them all, but as if
he lived in another country. There was nothing
but the square of sand he squatted on.
Flying was a prick of recognition gone foreign,
then a nagging absence, swallowed up by the wind.
Hour by hour, he became that emptiness,

just a breathing thing on the moving sand.
And then the line dividing the pulse
from the intake of air,
air ruffling feathers he no longer felt.

Cleopatra Mathis
White Sea
Sarabande Books

Huge Fragility

Osseous, osseous, osseous are the gulls, is the greatness
of the whitecapped ocean, the gulls like whitecaps pivoting toward the cove,
the whitecaps like gulls that curtsy toward me in fleets of fleece,
of frigid blue water, frigid and pitch and augmented by the unknown
and the blaring wind in coercion with the sea,
vast and cantankerous and in coercion with the sky,
those innocuous little clouds that so baroquely reside as if applied freshly,
the oil of flesh and white, never quite
brittle, the leafless hedges that barricade the shoreline
in contrast to my humanness, flesh and white, never quite
a part of the formidable arrangement of land and sea and flying whitecaps.
I can't locate any point of identity, no plane of reference
to place myself in this prosaic setting if only more prosaically
as in a snapshot of it not taken, not remembered, not saved, not forgotten,
within the landscape that alters cheaply, like the metallic eyes
of a crucified Christ, which open then shut
depending upon which way you lean, left or right,
except for the vanishing point of the pencil-thin horizon
arbitrarily drawn to landmark eternity, a chalk-drawn finish line
that lends sufficient emphasis to the marvelous ruse of my immortality
with its excessive blarney or blatant lack-of, cruelly blanketed
in the whetted edge of frigid blue water
and pavilion of gulls in their pawky contrivance
of heavenly ascension.

Tory Dent
Black Milk
The Sheep Meadow Press

Hummingbird

We buried the hummingbird
in his mantle of light, buried
him deep in the loam, one eye
staring into the earth's fiery
core, the other up through
the door in the sky. His needle
beak pointed east, his curled
feet west, and we each touched
our fingertips to his breast
before lifting them up from
the darkness to kiss. And
from our blessed fists we
rained the powdery dirt
down, erasing the folded
wings, the dream-colored
head, tamping the torn grass
with the heels of our hands,
our bare feet, summer almost
over, swaying together on the great
ship of death as clouds sailed by,
blowing our hair and the wind
walked us back to our room.

Dorianne Laux
Cairn 39
Spring 2005

Sand

It's not mine
but I should have seen it coming –
the gradual pulverizing – you know,
eventually it will all disappear,
as will you.
I did not mean for everything
to get smaller.
I did not mean for the rich, richer
and the poor, poorer,
nor for everything to be fair
though my translators
bandy about "justice" and "righteousness"
with abandon
as though words were meant to correlate to thoughts.
As though ideas matter.
And things matter.
Do dunes compensate?
I did not invent intent.
You did.
And the way indented footprints disappear
on the ocean's arrival?
That was yours, too.
How eloquent.

Patty Seyburn
Image
Art • Faith • Mystery
Number #47
Fall 2005

Late Beauty

(Saint Augustine, *Confessions*, Book X)

A shimmer of doves over the canyon of 116th Street:
they are like the fraying of the dark edge of concentration
against the brilliance of this earthly light,
not the birds themselves, but only their images
above a winter landscape supine, withdrawn,
still undeceived by the vernal miracle.
> *I have learnt to love you late,*
> *Beauty at once so ancient and so new!*
> *I have learnt to love you late!*

They divide into two bodies above the broken tenement,
like wings of barley flung votive into the flame
of a hunger not yet conscious of itself.
Augustine asks, Must we know God before we can pray?
I know they are raised on the tenement rooftops for food.
They return to their throne in the north by the light of day.
> *I have learnt to love you late,*
> *Beauty at once so ancient and so new!*
> *I have learnt to love you late!*

They wheel in silence, a shakedown, an evanescence.
They plead with the light itself like an undulant prayer:
Not what I once was, but what I am now.
In their stalled phalanx they veer, as at the blow of a hand.
a body manifold on the unresisting air,
the bodies of my parents in this light that fails.
> *I have learnt to love you late,*
> *Beauty at once so ancient and so new!*
> *I have learnt to love you late!*

Every morning I wake to the voices of doves
in the courtyard and my neighbor's Gregorian chant:
the vulgar murmur and the music of praise.
A bull-necked male performs a little hopping dance,
his rainbow wattles throbbing. In a gray glare of wings,
the round-eyed, soiled incarnation is complete.

   I have learnt to love you late,
   Beauty at once so ancient and so new!
   I have learnt to love you late!

"What would you have words do?" a poet asked me,
"and is it the same thing as what you would have your life do?"
The sounds of their names in my memory:
these things have passed through the air and are no more.
Light, the queen of colors, in a hollow sanctuary.
Yet–not an image, but something in its own right, then.

   I have learnt to love you late,
   Beauty at once so ancient and so new!
   I have learnt to love you late!

And Nabokov writes of the descent of a petal
from a blossoming tree that its single reflection
rose to meet it in the water more quickly
than the blossom fell. He says the union took place
"with the magic precision of a poet's word
meeting halfway his, or a reader's, recollection."

   I have learnt to love you late,
   Beauty at once so ancient and so new!
   I have learnt to love you late!

Again, again, they waver like a sleeve
shrugged back from a hand writing in the silence,
metaphor the broken halves of a single body,
rhyme the broken halves of a single sound.
Who has the power to loose them over the water,
after forty days of rain?

   I have learnt to love you late,
   Beauty at once so ancient and so new!
   I have learnt to love you late!

They wink at the eye that sees them, and always beauty
is just ahead: the rejection, the falling petal,
ghosts of phosphorus and snow in the broken meander
of cornices. Then the light retires once more;
they flee to the hand that freed them; the sky is empty.
But the prayer is in the praise.

Karl Kirchwey
At the Palace of Jove
G. P. Putnam's Sons

Honey Suckles

In caves created by waves of wild rose
small furry babes croon through
their first summer of perfume and excess

Trestles stamped *RAILROAD PROPERTY*
stagger under dusty vine

Such succulent prosperity intertwines
that gooseberry inflation
o'er-juices the track

Bees from one engorged economy
buzz back and forth to the next

And the wind from off your loaded freight
shafts past this vegetable luxe
making a visible crease in creation

Your stung senses strain
to divine such interwoven immensity

Pollen undoes regulation
Touch verges on trade
Wild factories braid futures

The blue morning-glory
(spent)
breaks off
only to catch
in blackberry nets

Daniel Wolff
Western Humanities Review
Volume LIX, Number 1
Spring 2005

Home Front and Gardens

Why am I standing here with this American Beauty, its roots
Wrapped up like a mummy's balls? If I could bury them,
These dry sticks would bleed through the whole hot summer.

But the snow's still soaking up the shadows, and the war's
Still fierce, though winding down like a dead turban.
You can't plant a rose bush where nothing dents the dirt.

What I need is a rush of rotors to sweep the ground,
And a bomb so far off target it blows a hole through winter
And frees the frozen earth for this drowsy stock.

And all I have is a shovel to lean on, like some
Frail philosopher lost in lazy theories of the grave,
None deep enough to reach where roses bank and burn.

Elton Glaser
Shenandoah
The Washington and Lee University Review
Volume 55, Number 3
Winter 2005

Twilight: After Haying

Yes, long shadows go out
from the bales; and yes, the soul
must part from the body:
what else could it do?

The men sprawl near the baler,
too tired to leave the field.
They talk and smoke,
and the tips of their cigarettes
blaze like small roses
in the night air. (It arrived
and settled among them
before they were aware.)

The moon comes
to count the bales,
and the dispossessed –
Whip-poor-will Whip-poor-will
– sings from the dusty stubble.

These things happen . . . the soul's bliss
and suffering are bound together
like the grasses . . . .

The last, sweet exhalations
of timothy and vetch
go out with the song of the bird;
the ravaged field
grows wet with dew.

Jane Kenyon
Collected Poems
Graywolf Press

Virgil: *from the Second Georgic*

O greatly fortunate farmers, if only they knew
How lucky they are! Far from the battlefield,
Earth brings forth from herself in ample justice
The simple means of life, simply enjoyed.
What if there's no great mansion from whose proud
High doors at dawn the crowd of those who came
The evening before to flatter the lord of the place
Pours out; what if the farmer has never gazed
In open-mouthed astonishment at such
Doors as those doors, adorned with tortoiseshell,
Or draperies tricked out with gold, or bronzes
Brought from Ephyraeus; what if no dye
Imported from Assyria has ever
Stained his pure white woolen cloth; what if
The clear plain daily olive oil he uses
Has never been sophisticated by
The mingling in of oil of cassia bark?
His sleep at night is easy, his life knows nothing
About deceit or trickery, and his life
Is rich in many things: tranquillity
Of the broad fields, of grottoes, and of lakes,
Of cattle lowing while in the shade of a tree
The herdsman peacefully dozes – they have all this –
They have forest glades, and haunts of beasts to hunt,
A youth accustomed to simplicity
And disciplined by work, respect for the elders,
And for the gods. When Justice left the earth,
She left her footprint here, among such people.

But as for me, oh may the gracious Muses,
Gracious beyond all else, whose holy emblems
I consecrated bear in the procession,
Grant me their favor and reveal to me
The courses of the stars above in the heavens;
Teach me about the sun in its eclipse,
And about the many labors of the moon;
What is it that causes quakings of the earth?
What force is it that suddenly makes the great
Sea rise and swell and break through all restraints
And then subside into itself again?
Why is it that the sun in winter hurries
To plunge itself into the sea and why
Is the winter night so slow to come to an end?
But if the blood around my heart's too cold
To gain me access to such mighty knowledge,
Then may I find delight in the rural fields
And the little brooks that make their way through valleys,
And in obscurity love the woods and rivers.
I long for such places, oh I long to be
By Spercheus or at Táygeta in Sparta
Where maidens celebrate the rites of Bacchus,
Or to be safe in the cool Haemian glade,
Protected in the shade of those great branches!

That man is blessed who has learned the causes of things,
And therefore under his feet subjugates fear
And the decrees of unrelenting fate
And the noise of Acheron's insatiable waters.
He too is happy who knows the country gods,
The sister Nymphs, and Pan, and old Sylvanus.
He's undisturbed by worldly honors, or by
The purple worn by kings, or by the strife
Of faithless brother fighting faithless brother,
Or by the leagued barbarians from the north,
The Dacians and their allies from the Danube,
Or by the skill of Roman power causing
Dynasties across the world to perish.
He neither looks with pity on the poor
Nor does he look with envy at the rich.
He takes from his fields and from his orchard boughs

What they have offered of their own free will,
Nor does he have experience of the iron
Hard-heartedness of the law, the Forum's madness,
Insolence of bureaucratic office.

There are those who with their oars disturb the waters
Of dangerous unknown seas, and those who rush
Against the sword, and those who insinuate
Their way into the chamber of a king;
There's the one who brings down ruin on a city
And all its wretched households, in his desire
To drink from an ornate cup and go to sleep
On Tyrian-purple coverlets at night;
There's the man who heaps up gold, and hides it away,
Hovering watchfully over it like a lover;
There's he who stares up stupefied at the Rostrum;
There's the open-mouthed undone astonishment
Of the one who hears the waves and waves of the wild
Applause of the close-packed crowd in the theater;
There are those who bathe in their brothers' blood, rejoicing;
And those who give up house and home for exile,
Seeking a land an alien sun shines on.

The farmer works the soil with his curved plow;
This is the work he does, and it sustains
His country, and his family, and his cattle,
His worthy bullocks and his herd of cows.
No rest from this, but the year will abound with fruits,
With newborn livestock, and with Ceres' sheaves
Filling the fields and overflowing the barn.
Then winter is coming: the olive press is turning;
The pigs come home well-fed, made happy by acorns;
The woods offer arbutus, and autumn yields
All its variety; high up, on the rocks,
The year's vintage mellows in the sunshine.
The farmer's simple house is pure and chaste.
His children gather around him for his kisses;
On the joyful lawn the little goats fight their battles,
Butting their horns; the cows' udders are full;
It's holiday time for the farmer: at ease on the grass,
With a fire going and friends wreathing the wine bowl,

He pours a libation, Bacchus, in honor of you,
While for the game of darts some of the shepherds
Put up a target on a nearby elm,
And others of them bare their sturdy limbs,
All ready for the rustic wrestling matches.

This is what it was like for the Sabines then,
And for Romulus and Remus, in the old days.
This must be how Etruria grew strong,
And Rome became the most beautiful thing there is,
One single wall surrounding seven hills.
Indeed, before the reign began of the king
Born on the Cretan mountain, and before
Impious men first feasted on slaughtered bullocks,
This is the way it was for golden Saturn,
Before the time when anyone had heard
The loud blare of a military trumpet
Or the clanging of a sword on the hard anvil.

Virgil
The Georgics of Virgil
A Translation by David Ferry
Farrar, Straus and Giroux

NOTE:

"Born on the Cretan mountain": Jupiter, said to have been born on the island of Crete.

Concerning a Young Woman

Like a blush pippin ripening on its branch,
the top-most branch, the very tip of a branch
the pickers overlooked – if not overlooked,
then at least so high it outreached their hooks.

*

Like wild hyacinth scattered on a mountain course,
their petals trampled as the shepherds pass
working back down through the lowland vales, the burst-
blue water-colored stains now flower in the dirt.

– Sappho

Sherod Santos
Greek Lyric Poetry:
A New Translation
W. W. Norton & Company

NOTE:

It may be difficult for a modern reader to fully appreciate how unusual Sappho's poetry was in its day, or how profoundly it marked the range and register of the lyric poem. In Hermogenes' *Kinds of Style*, Sappho's work is admired for its ability "to describe in simple terms pleasures that are not base, the beauty of a place, for example, the variety of plant life, the diversity of streams, and so on." But what distinguishes her from other poets who share this respect for the natural world is how she used that world to exalt the full range of her fervent and uncommon passions. In *Orations*, Themistius observes: "We allow Sappho... to be immoderate and excessive in praise of the beloved, for loved and lover were both private individuals, and there was no danger in it if the loved ones should become elevated by praise. For this love has a nobility, and noble the beloved." So admired was Sappho's work that Plato ordained her "the tenth muse," and Plutarch in *Virtues of Women* forswore the usual equivocations in ranking women poets: "if we show, by comparing Sappho's poems with Anacreon's... that the art of poetry... is not one art when practiced by men and another when practiced by women but is the same, will anyone be able to find just cause for blame in our demonstration?" Surely few poets in history have attracted such a distinguished list of poet-translators: Hardy, Shelley, Dante Gabriel Rosetti, Byron, Housman, Tennyson, and Swinburne among them.

The Spanish Lover

There were warnings: he had, at forty, never
married; he was too close to his mother,
calling her by her given name, *Manuela,*
ah, Manuela – like a lover; even her face

had bled, even the walls, giving birth to him;
she still had saved all of his baby teeth
except the one he had yet to lose, a small
eyetooth embedded, stubborn in the gum.

I would eat an artichoke down to its heart,
then feed the heart to him. It was enough
that he was not you – and utterly foreign,
related to no one. So it was not love.

So it ended badly, but to some relief.
I was again alone in my bed, but not
invisible as I had been to you –
and I had learned that when I drank sherry

I was drinking a chalk-white landscape, a distant
poor soil; that such vines have to suffer; and that
champagne can be kept effervescent by putting
a knife in the open mouth of the bottle.

Claudia Emerson
Late Wife
Louisiana State University Press

Oasis

We found (like the deserting) spacious calm,
drank a pair of Arnold Palmers underneath a palm.
Went for massage and mud, lacquer, love,
overheated minerals, a stimulating rub.
Then – as if it could be used, as if for art –
I placed a grain of doubt in your open-pored heart,
and watched what had been small dilate
and everything else evaporate.

Dana Goodyear
Honey and Junk
W. W. Norton & Company

First Love

They say
the first love's most important.
That's very romantic,
but not my experience.

Something was and wasn't there between us,
something went on and went away.

My hands never tremble
when I stumble on silly keepsakes
and a sheaf of letters tied with string
– not even ribbon.

Our only meeting after years:
two chairs chatting
at a chilly table.

Other loves
still breathe deep inside me.
This one's too short of breath even to sigh.

Yet just exactly as it is,
it does what the others still can't manage:
unremembered,
not even seen in dreams,
it introduces me to death.

Wisława Szymborska
Translated from the Polish by
Clare Cavanagh and Stanisław Barańczak
Monologue of a Dog
Harcourt, Inc.

Latents

Just the hints, say
the side ridges of
fingerprints that
don't rule out
innocence; or
the loose approaches
to tightening mazes;
ambiguous, smudgy
places. The dilation
dark absorbs; the
thing we don't
think through
before it happens:
all the early
stations of desire –
the first slight tug
against the string
that threads the
wire that threads
the cable that
guys the bridge
that alien traffic
plies.

Kay Ryan
The Niagara River
Grove Press

Lesser Evils

After a morning of work in separate rooms
she said she was going to the municipal pool
and he said he would walk along the river
for a while before they met back for their lunch
of tomatoes and cheese. But in fact she went
to the lobby of the Hotel du Panthéon
to read the *Herald Tribune* and drink a cup
of the Irish tea she liked and he to
the little church of St. Médard. A couple
old women in housedresses knelt in the first pews.
He sat in the back, with the drunks or alone.
And at lunch she said terrible, the lanes
were filled with kids from the elementary school
or terrific, I had it to myself. And he said
a barge full of oyster shells. Then quiet sex
with the curtains drawn against the chemistry
students conducting their experiments in the building
across the street. Incremental triumphs
of exactitude and necessity. In the evenings
they liked to fire champagne corks over at the vast
darkened laboratory windows. Imagining the mice
startling in their cages, imagining catastrophe.
Turning back to their tumors with relief.

Joel Brouwer
Poetry
Volume CLXXXVII, Number 3
December 2005

Marvell Noir

Sweetheart, if we had the time,
A week in bed would be no crime.
I'd light your Camels, pour your Jack;
You'd do shiatsu on my back.
When you got up to scramble eggs,
I'd write a sonnet to your legs,
And you could watch my stubble grow.
Yes, gorgeous, we'd take it slow.
I'd hear the whole sad tale again:
A roadhouse band; you can't trust men;
He set you up; you had to eat,
And bitter with the bittersweet
Was what they dished you; Ginger lied;
You weren't there when Sanchez died;
You didn't know the pearls were fake . . .
Aw, can it, sport! Make no mistake,
You're in it, doll, up to your eyeballs!
Tears? Please! You'll dilute our highballs,
And make that angel face a mess
For the nice Lieutenant. I confess
I'm nuts for you–but take the rap?
You must think I'm some other sap!
And, precious, I kind of wish I was.
Well, when they spring you, give a buzz;
Guess I'll get back to Archie's wife,
And you'll get twenty-five to life.
You'll have time then, more than enough,
To reminisce about the stuff
That dreams are made of and the men
You suckered. Sadly, in the pen
Your kind of talent goes to waste.
But Irish bars are more my taste
Than iron ones: stripes ain't my style.
You're going down; I promise I'll
Come visit every other year.
Now kiss me, sweet–the squad car's here.

Ann Lauinger
Parnassus: Poetry in Review
Volume 28, No. 1 & No. 2

Travel Plans

The pepper tree spilled round us from its source,
and took a lumpish this-way, that-way course,
while dangling hopeful sprays of cinnabar.
You couldn't rest against the grizzled trunk;
its bulby hump, its knurled and craggy scar,
forced you to lean your weight on me instead.
The two of us were just a little drunk,
and sipped the sun-warmed wine to make us bold.

"I'd like to go to Mexico," you said,
"with you, someday, before we're too damn old,"
while in the sky an airplane's vapor trail
politely licked its seal across the sun.
We watched the growing, tantalizing tail,
until it matter-of-factly came undone.

Leslie Monsour
The Alarming Beauty of the Sky
Red Hen Press

Animal Self

Rabbit, possum, skunk, raccoon, or deer:
our first winter morning in a new house
finds me searching our snowy yard for traces

of them again after a lifetime. No
longer a Tenderfoot reading the signs
up north in Minnesota, the woods closer

here than there, I figure the boy I was
would come as far up on the man I am
as I do now on my Green Giant shadow

thrown by the ground-hugging sun. When I seek
the creatures of the night, I track the kind
of animal I've grown into that leaves

footprints on a sheet of snow & brings
to light the dark – us two down on all fours.

Randy Blasing
Michigan Quarterly Review
Volume XLIV, No. 3
Summer 2005

Medical Advice

Kisses shorten life; mixing strange spittle
Or sucking in microbes, dozing under small flaps
Of gum or carelessly grazing on the plankton
Of teeth upsets the ecology of the mouth.

One could, of course, wear a surgical mask
And agree not to exhale while gauze touched
Gauze, or write letters from a distance
Disinfecting the pen and using self
Sealing envelopes for safety.

Some, I know, blinded by passion shed their
Clothes like children, pressing nakedness
To nakedness, making contact at all points
Throwing caution to the wind or worse.

A few die early from inhaled infection that
Turns plump hearts into prunes before their
Time, that withers the skin and blanks the
Brightness of the eye. They are love's martyrs.

Others with strong constitutions survive. Nursing
Injuries like war wounds, they limp through
Marriage, frequently resting on the shoulders
Of their love, while the cautious live to a ripe old
Age, camouflaging internal bleeding as late periods.

Joe Sheerin
Elves in the Wainscotting
Carcanet Press

Sounding Aboard the Rafaella

She loved me as the freeloading sea
Gulls love the slipstream of a mammoth hull.
It was her passion, this lack of need for me.
She let her resistance fall like an empire, her clothes like a tyrant's
Head: momentous and kindling, like no fire since.

And I loved her in the lull
Between vessels, in the tenselessness of an unbroken
Breaker, in the two mouths where one tongue was spoken.
The freighter's engine throbs against its cage
Of ocean, and my heart wrecks against this page.

Rex Wilder
Waking Bodies
Red Hen Press

The Welcome

Do you wish to immigrate to my heart? Where are your papers? What are your purposes?

Are you lost? Are you broken? Come to the chamber of my heart for safety. Remember the old country. I was not there. I was waiting for you here.

Do you wish to be naturalized in my arms? Let me instruct you in the new tongue. Tread softly; Death too first makes inquiry, then shows the way.

Come, pledge allegiance to my tattered proud flag. Here, and here only, the streets are paved with gold.

David Joel Friedman
The Welcome
University of Illinois Press

Re-gifting

Found: in *Title Page – Used and New Books,*
Rosemont, PA, a translation by Vladimir Nabokov
of poems by Pushkin, Tyntchev and Lermentov,
published London, 1947. A snip at twenty bucks.

Given for a 50th, to "my Boris more-than-Godunov"
from Anna, "Because of Pushkin, because of love";
then again, in 1986, to "my dear Joseph
who, tomorrow, will be heading off
to Moscow. From Alex. P.S. see above".

Vona Groarke
Verse
Volume 22, Number 1 – 2005

Oatmeal

Dry slide of Bob's Red Mill
Extra Thick Rolled Oats
off the scoop –

tiny dustcloud
settling like ash
from stirred coals.

Waking together,
happy, not
our first try.

Peggy Shumaker
The Iowa Review
Volume 35, Number 1
Spring 2005

13 Haiku About My Husband and Current State of Happiness

he has a lizard
in his mouth   it flicks   it flicks
seismic me he sends

i understand how
  to conduct a proper love affair
on paper

medium pasta shells garlic cheese broccoli saturday dinner

i caught my husband
        pretending to be a fly
                buzzing around shit

          i love my husband's

          pajama bottoms i en-

          vision his demise

wounded prehistoric beasts whine or
a husband practices trumpet

hot tea milk and honey hot tea milk and honey hot tea milk and hon

      i did not paint you
          while i dreamt about albert
      goldbarth i did not

happy all day i   have been leaping off of fat   margins into

                                                      space

scream into snowbanks you get
fogged glasses also great views of nothing

he smokes smells lets out
noxious fumes from his butt hole
wrinkled by much use

i caught my husband again buzzing near the trash in his underwear

          he has a good face
          i love him even as i
          buy life insurance

Mary Kane
Beloit Poetry Journal
Volume 56, Number 2
Winter 2005/06

Anent the Yellow Field, Fa-La

The blue that made the grassblades green
withdrew, and under clouds too cold for rain,
despicable, as she who loves and loathes me
says I am, I trudged the undergrowth, my song
a shame to no one in particular: fa-la: a ditty
without meaning, of no use. Where brittle, wan
with rime, the wood rush wasted underfoot,
sang I my nonsense sagely to myself: fa-la.

Brooks Haxton
TriQuarterly 121

A Marriage Must Be Worked At

Newlyweds on the honeymoon trip,
they are trying to get
from one set of ruins to the next.
There were no double berths.
He took the top.
Now they are three feet apart.
Neither sleeping.

They are perfectly still,
hurtling over the landscape.

Michael Chitwood
Crazyhorse
Number 68
Fall 2005

Anatomy of Failure

Shadows passed over the statues in the night –
crossed them, hesitated, vanished;
even the dust was white as a bird.

Someone had loved me, had
stopped loving me. I had
failed in a minute but final way;

all the words exchanged
risen past the boundaries
of what had been made

and what wasn't yet outlined, risen
like a parrot toward a sky
only to find a painted ceiling and a stenciled sun.

I lived in a museum, slept
up against a body of stone,
spine to block-grey base

as a stranger's face looked
down upon me,
a bird in someone else's mind.

Meghan O'Rourke
The New Republic
February 27, 2006

And Day Brought Back My Night

It was so simple: you came back to me
And I was happy. Nothing seemed to matter
But that. That you had gone away from me
And lived for days with him – it didn't matter.
That I had been left to care for our old dog
And house alone – couldn't have mattered less!
On all this, you and I and our happy dog
Agreed. We slept. The world was worriless.

I woke in the morning, brimming with old joys
Till the fact-checker showed up, late, for work
And started in: *Item: It's years, not days.*
Item: you had no dog. Item: she isn't back,
In fact, she just remarried. And oh yes, item: you
Left her, remember? I did? I did. (I do.)

Geoffrey Brock
Weighing Light
Ivan R. Dee, Publisher

The Long Marriage

They could not believe their luck – sunlight all the way down, lighting rocks lodged in the sandy bottom as if from within. Each rock angled just so, by some immense but casual intelligence. Rock weed held out its dark green fingers, waving. How can the water be so clear, and full of salt? In between their visits someone had removed the used condoms and shattered beer glass from the concrete cubicles, the breakwater fronting the old factory. *The olfactory*, he said. She did not see the humor.

At the beach a group gathered around the harbor seal who had hauled herself a small way onto the shore, waving an aristocratic flipper in the sun. Can't a mammal have a bit of privacy? She knew the feeling. The vertebra he plucked from the sand and showed her proudly was smooth, and cleanest white. But she would not have it in the house. Be happy you are alive and moving, she said. Bones belong in sand, rocks on ocean floor, and mercy in the great, shadowy hands of the indifferent one.

Jeffrey Skinner
Salt Water Amnesia
Ausable Press

Takeoff

We didn't fall out of love,
old love, we rose – we rose
as in a plane, as in the moment
when the wheels lift
and the whole craft
shudders against the gravity
it then forgets as
all at once the runway's
fretful rushing by the window
slows and resolves to field
and tree line, the beaten
metal of a pond
the sun anneals;

we rose the way it all
grows clearer
as it diminishes till
a car drives in place
along a road that winds
and straightens, straightens to wind
again across a widening
landscape in which
nothing at all is moving
except the ever-
smaller sharper
shadow of our
getting clear of it.

Alan Shapiro
Tantalus in Love
Houghton Mifflin Company

The Hoopoe's Crown

I suppose it's something I should embrace:
how a one-time sighting of a feathered crown –
before it's even recorded – becomes a treatise

on suffering and human limitation.
I couldn't remember one particular
of the legend of the hoopoe and King Solomon

only (from the picture) the fiery color,
how the fanned-out feathers *do* contrive a crown.
It was always my weakness – the spectacular –

I'd never have made the same request as Solomon.
For one thing, his judgments leave me cold;
I don't believe the world contains a woman –

real mother or not – who would have settled
for half the body of a divided infant,
or fall for such a threat: a child killed?

If this is wisdom's highest achievement,
it has to be a fairly hollow thing.
And then, when you consider its denouement:

how the man we acknowledge as our wisest king
finished up his life worshipping idols.
But I'm ahead of myself; I was telling

or planning to tell some old Near Eastern riddles,
like how the hoopoe got his feathered crown.
Solomon *is* involved; it's he who straddles

an earlier riddle's eagle, on a mission
to explore the farthest reaches of his kingdom.
But he's failed to factor in the pounding sun

(apparently, the refinements of his wisdom
don't extend themselves to head coverings).
The tale: a flock of hoopoes flies straight over him

and makes a canopy of outspread wings,
shading him for his entire expedition.
In my version, each pair of hoopoes sings

an ornate variation on a two-part canon
(from these, the Song of Songs will be compiled)
alternating wingbeats so no drop of sun

can penetrate the airy, makeshift shield.
A crown is the hoopoe's chosen reward,
and, against all warnings, he wants it gold.

Needless to say, he's mercilessly snared
for the easy, precious bounty on his head
until, his numbers dwindling, the humbled bird

accepts a crown of feathers in its stead,
which is where I begin to take an interest:
potential evidence, or, at least, a lead

in my increasingly maniacal quest
for even an inkling of divine collusion
in the bauble, the ornament, the *beau geste* –

something unaccounted for by evolution.
And don't try to tell me that the frivolous,
by definition, needs no justification.

I'm finding that you can't stave off unhappiness
by obsessive fussing over a hoopoe's crown;
probably, it's just too late for this.

I should have dashed it off that afternoon
still reeling from the heady dose of grace:
a garden overlooking the Mediterranean

my family pretending to be as rapturous
as I was when a pair of orange wings
landed right beside us on the grass.

Then, I might have done without the meanings,
but I thought I'd use that hoopoe as an overture:
I'd find the forgotten folktale, reread Kings –

crazy – when I'd just witnessed a creature
so much like a product of sheer artifice
I had to reconceive my notion of nature,

especially in that rumor-driven place
(this was the land of Israel, just north of Akko)
and, clearly, Whoever had made this bird for us

was a thorough devotee of pure rococo.
That should have been the revelation.
Why assume that something must have gone askew

if a bird wears an orange-feathered crown?
Imbibe some cockamamie explanation
about a king on an eagle in the baking sun?

Why not revel in ornamentation?
Clearly – look at the Temple – that's what Solomon did
for all his genius at deliberation,

and his was a wisdom straight from God,
who, with His typical lack of foresight,
threw in every other prize he had

until He'd made His own will obsolete:
immense riches, lands, power, women.
But if you ask me, Solomon was no more astute

than a bird tempting hunters with a crown.
Wasn't each gold cherub on the gold facade
of his over-the-top temple an invitation

to local thugs to plunder and maraud?
And isn't it, itself, a kind of idolatry –
all that gold, ivory, cedar, acacia wood –

or, at the very least, the height of folly?
The heaven's my throne, the earth's my footstool
(this is God talking) *what house can you build Me?*

I'm sorry. But Solomon's a fool.
Unless – he *was* wise, wasn't he? – he always knew
that all that admittedly absurd detail

was, frankly, the best that he could do.
Poor guy. It was faith he should have asked for;
think of the heartache of going through

that ridiculous charade, to manufacture
a vast and necessarily empty place.
Not that he thought extravagant expenditure

would replace faith – he wasn't fatuous –
but maybe he allowed himself the sneaking hope
that all that complicated enterprise

would, in its intensity, catch him up
and he'd find himself, in all its glare, believing.
Isn't that what I think . . . when I take up

some crazy subject . . . and try to make it sing?
I keep thinking, this time, I'll get it all:
not just the hoopoe's crown, the orange wing,

that headcase Solomon, the Hebrew Bible,
but my own lostness, without explaining
even a single miserable detail.

But I'll also forget some vital covering,
and what flock of birds would bail me out?
Believe me, I'll take sparrows, starlings, anything

or better still – but here I'm pushing it;
since it's not as if I have a crown to give –
I'd trade the whole flock for even brief delight

on my husband's face – I won't say love,
since his is so entwined with bitterness,
and, at best, completely uncommunicative,

except that day, with the hoopoe on the grass
when he seemed to take such pleasure in my pleasure
along with our three daughters – was it avarice

on my part? Should a wife and mother
let her family indulge her in that way?
He even managed to get a picture

of my hoopoe just before he flew away,
perhaps to make some king another canopy?
It's on a diskette somewhere, stashed away.

Who knows? Maybe, if I asked him for a copy,
he'd actually be glad to print one out.
He'd be happy for a minute. I'd be happy.

But I don't believe it; in fact, I doubt
he wants anything more than to be left alone.
So what choice do I have? I'm about

to do precisely that, for the duration,
when for years, I regretted that a mere lifetime
was all we'd have. I'm overthrown,

though I was full of love and faith; I still am
but it doesn't look like either one can save me.
Clearly, the thing I lack is wisdom,

not to mention a feathery canopy
to shield me from a brutal, brutal sun.
I suppose I, too, am just too greedy,

like that colossal fuck-up, Solomon
and his vainglorious bird. My loving family
has been – a bit too much – my golden crown

and it was spectacular, if only briefly.
No feathers to replace it, only pain,
which I, like an idiot, thought poetry

might be able to help me undermine.
No luck. But I have learned something;
it's a bankrupt business, ornamentation,

idolatrous, at worst; at best, an aching
absence of whatever it is that matters.
A little wisdom is a relentless thing;

everywhere I look, something shatters.
And as for that protective flock of stunning birds,
I don't envy Solomon when it scatters.

Jacqueline Osherow
The Hoopoe's Crown
BOA Editions, Ltd.

Acrostic: Outhouse

Once this homestead held many children,
uncles and great-uncles, delicate and stooping aunts
tatting lace all day, needles replacing
husbands who disappeared into Bayonet Woods, never returning,
obsession becoming gems of fine knots
until their men thread wholly into white roses,
sadly filigreed, as the wild roses
edging the outhouse are eaten by beetles.

Paula Bohince
Beloit Poetry Journal
Volume 56, Number 3
Spring 2006

First Breath Last Breath

When a baby boy is born
   and the midwife
      holds him up
  as he takes
     his first breath,
Place him over
   the mother's face
     so when the baby exhales
his first breath on Earth
    the mother breathes it.

And when the mother dies
   her middle-aged son
      the baby grew up to be,
  by her side
     his head next to her head,
Follows her breathing with his breath
   as it becomes shorter
     and as the dying mother
  exhales her last breath
    her son inhales it.

Antler
Denver Quarterly
Volume 40, Number 1
2005

At Home

Father was eating partridge and Mother was out
and I and Joris were talking about murders
and getaways and on what trains
when the sun rolled into our attic
and lay there gleaming in the hay.
Father swore and said: God sees me.
Joris made his getaway
and I went on playing with the trains
which ran on electricity across the floor
between posts.

Hugo Claus
Translated from the Dutch by John Irons
Greetings: Selected Poems
Harcourt, Inc.

A Lamb by Its Ma

Just before it rains, the lilacs
thrash weakly,
storm light heightening
the clusters drooping
at their peak of scent,
wind running
through them like slow water,
then a splash, mood swing:
leaves spangled with drops
from inside the storm.
Mary made us come inside
if there was lightning,
flapping a white towel
to call us back.
We hung around the kitchen
drinking tea till it cleared.
She brought us tea at bedtime.
A good cup of black tea
and you'll sleep like a lamb by its ma.
She told us that our parents
loved us, that their war
was theirs alone.
She said it in the charged air,
in the scent of their absence
from the house,
their clean absence.
If thunder came at night,
she told about the brave
and faithful dogs of Scotland,
how a shepherd knows
where his lamb has gone
by bits of wool in the wire.

Chase Twichell
Dog Language
Copper Canyon Press

Horseneck Beach Odalisque

Gunmetal blue, then iris blue, then turquoise,
the plain of the Atlantic burned to steel
that summer along the Horseneck.
Our castles rose, dark and raggedly Gothic.
The dribbled turrets capped a moated wall,
and then the Muslim tide came roiling in
and took the holy cities one by one.
By August we were Moor-wasps,
each boy a white-toweled sultan of the waves.
Sand crabs scrabbled from our tightened palms,
burrowing downward through the pooling muck
to the icy realm of salt and shell. Each footprint
bred an archipelago. Across the boiling lagoon
of August, Martha's Vineyard reigned,
a bruised thumb above the feathery caps.
Mother was our harem, our peasantry.
Beside us a grand vizier on his crimson towel
(the New Bedford lawyer, his back a twisted hump)
sat patiently and watched the sunset come.

William Logan
The Whispering Gallery
Penguin Books

Absence

Talking to the children's absence, you imagine them
canoeing or sitting before a fire, sparks

arcing like imitation stars. There's so much to say,
even in the unrelenting heat, the sun

balanced overhead while you collect facts for them
as if they can hear you: how the barracuda's jaw

can spread so wide then thrash and rip into anything,
how bees can't find their hive if it's moved

more than a few inches, how your own house settles
fraction by fraction into clay and river stone,

and dust is alive though you sweep it into piles
meaning the desert is a guest in the corner

of your room, meaning your feet keep stirring clouds
of creatures and you pass over animal and plant

and never feel the burden, or do feel the burden and bend
like a sapling, like a heavy flower brushing

the ground. This is what separation trains you for.
You as an envelope releasing them, you ripping

the cord, you with your stains on them, the ones
you need ten hundred mirrors

to see. The old goddess of tether and straw, the one
who makes you to lie down, to be crushed

till you come out oil of fish, oil of granite, come out
ash and live in the fine grit under their feet,

who licked you alive and left the taste in your own mouth,
your own love: sand, ground tooth, spider,

sawdust, hair, and adoration turned to powder,
and absence teaching its teaching and all

you cannot say, you'll never say, swallowed, a coating
inside lungs and all passageways, all orifices being

the openings of absence, and what you want to say turns
to air, but you try your prayer once more: old goddess

of rain, wash us with your silent tongue as if
we were always being born, just born, slick

and stunned, with our legs kicking

Anne Marie Macari
Gloryland
Alice James Books

Obedience, or The Lying Tale

I will do everything you tell me, Mother.
I will charm three gold hairs
from the demon's head.
I will choke the mouse that gnaws
an apple tree's roots and keep its skin
for a glove. To the wolf, I will be
pretty and kind, and curtsy
his crossing of my path.

The forest, vocal
even in its somber tread, rages.
A slope ends in a pit of foxes
drunk on rotten brambles of berries,
and the raccoons ransack
a rabbit's unmasked hole.
What do they find but a winter's heap
of droppings? A stolen nest, the cracked shell

of another creature's child.
I imagine this is the rabbit way,
and I will not stray, Mother,
into the forest's thick,
where the trees meet the dark,
though I have known misgivings
of light as a hot hand that flickers
against my neck. The path ends

at a river I must cross. I will wait
for the ferryman
to motion me through. Into the waves,
he etches with his oar
a new story: a silent girl runs away,
a silent girl is never safe.
I will take his oar in my hand. I will learn
the boat's rocking and bring myself back

and forth. To be good
is the hurricane of caution.
I will know indecision's rowing,
the water I lap into my lap
as he shakes his withered head.
Behind me is the forest. Before me
the field, a loose run of grass. I stay
in the river, Mother, I study escape.

Jennifer Chang
Virginia Quarterly Review
Volume 81, Number 4
Fall 2005

My Mother's Hands

Now that she's ashamed of their ancient burls and gibbous knobs —
"Don't be ashamed!" I cry —
I find myself staring at the raw matter of their decay,
nails crumbling to the opalescent grit
of their lunulae, liver spots speckling the dorsal vein
with its throbbing blue limbs, as if the leopard,
symbol of lust in Dante, lay panting, enfeebled,
in the dark wood.

I can't bear that these hands won't always be here,
though I barely noticed them when they were still dexterous,
commanding me to come here, do this chore, listen to this
sweet story, come here, sweetheart, come here . . .

Now a scythelike rod planted within the same index finger
gives it an incongruous come-hither look that forces
passersby to point to themselves, thinking
she's beckoning to them, an optical illusion, of course,
like the Beauty and the Crone.

"This hand is not the crux and matter of you," I want to say,
but know she'd laugh and ask, "Is it what's the matter
with you?" or — worse — look away in pain, saying,
"It doesn't matter, it doesn't matter."

And so I hold on tight as she sits in her wheelchair, as if
to guide her somewhere, anywhere, until I kiss her goodbye,
and her hands fall from my own to a spot on her desk
by the gift my father gave her when they were young:
a glass paperweight, clear, abstract, voluptuous,
with five sparkling air bubbles clutching
a bouquet of clouds.

David Woo
The Eclipses
BOA Editions, Ltd.

Near Hag's Head

(Cliffs of Moher, Ireland)

This headland is the battered prow
of a ship my silent father rides
into the Atlantic. Gust after gust
buffets the raw crag of his face,
his windbreaker flapping like a sail.

He could be his own father's grandfather
the way he stands before the rail
as others stood before the hold, the blind
journey before them, and nods to me
in recognition despite the ocean between us.

Even he knows on these cliffs the dead
are reading aloud from the book of the wind.

Daniel Tobin
The Narrows
Four Way Books

Peter Street

I'd grown almost to love this street,
each time I passed looking up
to pin my father's face to a window, feel myself

held in his gaze. Today there's a building site
where the hospital stood and I stop and stare
stupidly at the empty air, looking for him.

I'd almost pray some ache remain
like a flaw in the structure, something unappeasable
waiting in the fabric, between floors, in some

obstinate, secret room. A crane moves
delicately in the sky, in its own language.
Forget all that, I think as I pass, make it

a marvellous house; music should roam the corridors,
joy readily occur, St Valentine's
stubborn heart come floating from Whitefriar Street

to prevail, to undo injury, to lift my father from his bed,
let him climb down the dull red brick, effortlessly,
and run off with his life in his hands.

Peter Sirr
Selected Poems
Wake Forest University Press

The United States

If you asked what it is all about
I would say a field a green field
in the turning rows a killdeer
and after that barbed wire
the hedge with its cardinals
a blacktop then another field

Corn   one of the main things
after water   and before milk
for whiskey is in it   and grits
gold for chickens   pearls before swine
there is a factory in every plant
if we could be properly humble

it is the greatness of the nation
along with cartoon animation
automobiles and rock 'n roll
jazz and basketball evolved here
but not one other U.S. God
just the corn's imperial row

on row then Sylvester Stallone
and airbrushed Elvis thank you
very much ladies and gentlemen
Presley Dylan and the Supremes
no I would say a field a vast field
at the center top-hogs and cattle

then art the cities New York
Chicago Houston Seattle man
told me last week experts can
teach starlings to talk   hell
televangelists may yet witness
in terza rima each stalk of corn

contributes it has been so
hybridized with its immense
ears it no longer resembles
maize it is what we have left
to barter for oil and microchips
tons of it siloed and elevated

to float us through droughts
and wars and speculations we ask
which will most cogently represent us
Leaves of Grass or *The Simpsons*
there is the idea that every
living thing is a subset of human

control and the other notion
that though we may go on
a few hundred or thousand
years the poison has spilled
no more land will be made
the search for another arable

planet may prove moot as the
search for earthly sentience
meanwhile this taco here
crunches in the great scheme of
things we persist one people one
of the potential fates of corn

Rodney Jones
Shenandoah
The Washington and Lee University Review
Volume 55, Number 2
Fall 2005

The Demise of Camembert

I remember my mother squeezing
the camembert. She bought it five days

before unwrapping it, unwrapped it
two hours before she served it.

But what the French sociologist calls
la déstructurisation of family meals

means there's no more patience
for ripening on the cold shelf.

This message comes to us
on a tray with quick-serve cheddar puffs

passed across the cocktail party,
across news networks via satellite.

Also it lands thudding with the flat bread,
bean salad, raisins, fruit bar,

seedless jam and plastic cutlery
in the humanitarian airdrop.

Pah! A man rejects the bland cheese couplets.
And the premoistened serviette.

In this world he fears annihilation.
This world has made him a nihilist.

Now he sits on a bed, on the bedspread
in a motel on the edge of Las Vegas

or a hotel near Narita Airport,
eating an engineered salty snack,

planning deaths designed his way,
getting more and more thirsty.

So hear me. Compassion begins in the pasture.
Adoration of cow breed, grass strain,

the certain season for milking,
the way the curd is cut and pressed

and salted and cured and shaped,
the time and temperature at each stage.

The marketing man from Coeur-de-Lion,
the number-one brand of camembert,

is revising the résumé of his ripe life.
And you and I, paring away the rind,

do you and I have a patient nose
for the creamy inwardness of things?

Ron Slate
The Incentive of the Maggot
A Mariner Original
Houghton Mifflin Company

Elena Ceauçescu's Bed

Making ourselves at home in that broad bed
    Elena left, we slept snug as the mouse
That, burrowing in guest room blankets, fed
    Her brood last winter in our summer house.

What bed, through all our lives long, had we known
    If not the tyrant's? How many had been driven
Homeless and hungering while I had my own
    Bed, my own room? How many have been given

Lives at hard labor while our markets rose
    And we had all we asked for in the lands
Of milk and honey? Where could you find those
    Who hunted, once, that hill where my house stands?

There'll be just one bed, too soon, for us all.
    What empire's hacked out by the meek, the kind?
The lioness kills; the lion feasts; the small
    Bury their noses in what's left behind.

W. D. Snodgrass
Not for Specialists:
New and Selected Poems
BOA Editions, Ltd.

A Stick, A Cup, A Bowl, A Comb

These were some of their laws:
These were a few of the miles they cruised:
Here is where their beds went down:
With this their fate was sealed:
These are some things they shared:
These were with what they were comforted:
In this manner were they made to be cared for:
In these ways were they shaped to be seen:
Among these things were what they could bear:
In this time here is what they will be shown:
With this will they be remembered:
These were some of their customs:
These were with what they kept to themselves:
Here is a place they questioned:
In this way were they asked to provide:
There were what they provided:
In these instances thus were they praised:
It was with this were they wondering:
These were with what they marked themselves:
With this will they be never forgotten:
These were some of their means:
Here is an example of one of their methods:
With this did they solace themselves:
With this did they adorn themselves:
In these ways did they keep their provisions:
This is what they did with what they were fond of:
By this practice did they shore up magnificence:
These were what they were asked to furnish:
They caused these things to be memorized:
These were their most common rituals:
Among these these were considered unnecessary:
And in these were they in surplus: These things they misused:
And prized:
And forfeited:
And pitied:
By these means did they resist their discovery:
These were some of the choices they made:
With these did they choose to be represented:

With these did they divine:
And with this were they occupied:
With these things did they labor:
For these things did they hope for:
For these did they say they would die for:
These were the bargains they struck:
This is what they were given in exchange:
This is how they recognized one another:
By these means was love aroused:
Here are fragments of what they worshipped:
Among these things they passed their days:
Here is what they were willing to sacrifice:
In the traces of these things they were known by:
This is what they have left:
Here is where they left without a trace:
These were some of their gifts:

Dara Wier
The Massachusetts Review
Volume 46, Number 2
Summer 2005

Board Book & the Costume
of a Whooping Crane

Two new words a day & sometimes three – *cup* & *doll*, yesterday *throat*
    & *hot, hot hot,*
the *T* extended, *hot-uh,* fingers drumming the radiator. He's thirteen months,
    hand to the windowsill,

head tilted up to glimpse a squirrel. Freshly changed, he squeals
    as inches from his face
the squirrel stares toward him, its eyes a shrouded planet, cloud cover
    seen from space,

monsoon roiling the Pacific. Then his brother, laughing, tackles him,
    squirrel leaping down to snow.
If learning is delight, then gnosis asks unshroudings more laborious,
    the hard unspooling,

the rended gauze. & everywhere the shrouds & everywhere
    the shrouds to come.
The President's rodent eye pulses out from CNN, darting & glazed,
    squinting for the next thing

to lift to the mouth, for he must eat & eat. As the boys sit down
    to sift through board books,
the grim hand jitters up from the podium, class ring
    in a dazzle of pixels.

Today he will entertain no questions, impatient for the killings to begin,
    executions to roll
on his tongue like acorns, berries purpling the gaping mouth.
    Already he can taste them.

Now the cutaway to ordnance & acronym, F-16s snarling up
    from a carrier, the MOAB
& its 21,000 pounds of murder. But here – a board book of cranes,
    open & aflutter in Luke's hands.

& now Jake joining him. *Touch & feel,* so his fingers stroke a tuft
    of feathers, orange rubbery
hieroglyphic of a foot. Sandhill Crane, Demoiselle Crane,
    Black-Crowned, Gray-Crowned,

Wattled & Blue, Sarus, Siberian, Hooded & White-Necked,
    Eurasian, Red-Crowned,
Australian & Eastern Sarus, & *Grus americana* – Whooping Crane,
    almost extinct for a century,

numbers dwindled by DDT, by power line & coyote, drought & poachers
    selling ground-up bills
to Beijing and Macao – an antidote for hair loss – until scarcely
    a hundred remain, hatched

& fledged in captivity. Also here, the photo I've tacked above my desk,
    a zoo attendant
in the costume of a whooping crane, cumbersome in bird mask,
    a parachute gathered

to make a kind of overall. He's bending to a nest of fledglings,
    beaks agape & waiting.
Released to the wild, few of them survive for long. The boys
    sift the pages, hands

brailling yellow beaks. The President hisses on, martial music
    seeping from marine band horns,
the snow in thickening spirals. I am suiting up, the costume
    clumsy as a spacesuit,

white silk billowing, the lemon-colored boots ridiculous clowns' feet.
    & the mask pasted tight
with sweat & the ache of my ascending. I sprout Ovidian claws,
    my eyes look down

on miles of stratosphere, the piston work of wing-beat
    & outstretched glide,
the long wail echoing from the throat, the fish within my jaws,
    struggling still, the circling,

the gyres diminishing to touchdown & my gangling
    stagger toward them
who will lavishly outlive me. & from my mouth this rainbow,
    wet & silvering.

David Wojahn
Interrogation Palace:
New and Selected Poems 1982-2004
University Of Pittsburgh Press

Blackbird

There was nothing I could have done –
a flurry of blackbirds burst
from the weeds at the edge of a field
and one veered out into my wheel
and went under. I had a moment
to hope he'd emerge as sometimes
they will from beneath the back
of the car and fly off,
but I saw him behind on the roadbed,
the shadowless sail of a wing
lifted vainly from the clumsy
bundle of matter he'd become.

There was nothing I could have done,
though perhaps I was distracted:
I'd been listening to news of the war,
hearing that what we'd suspected
were lies had proved to be lies,
that many were dying for those lies,
but as usual now, it wouldn't matter.
I'd been thinking of Lincoln's,
". . . You can't fool all of the people
all of the time . . ." how I once
took comfort from the hope and trust
it implied, but no longer.

I had to slow down now,
a tractor hauling a load of hay
was approaching on the narrow lane.
The farmer and I gave way and waved:
the high-piled bales swayed
menacingly over my head but held.
Out in the newly harvested fields,

already harrowed and raw,
more blackbirds, uncountable
clouds of them, rose, held
for an instant, then broke,
scattered as though by a gale.

C. K. Williams
AGNI 61

Contract Law

If every exchange is negotiated with the presumption of bad faith,
the only possible way to come away with even a piece of what you
want is to propose basic terms which you have no intention of fulfilling,
while feeling around for what givens on the other side can be seized
and services extracted without further harm to you, though the tenets
of the system be destroyed. Thus one does real business with family,
from whom there is no extraction, and on whom survival often depends,
so is neo-sacralized, while any outside encounter provides opportunities
for real advancement on terms that can be as fresh as one's devising,
with no disturbance to the interior life. This is a failure of contract law,
a primary means of exclusion, and an aspect of state failure in general,
along with environmental depredation, disputes over birth rates,
and thousands of incalculable daily forms of threat and coercion,
culminating in violent deaths that achieve sporadic documentation.

Michael Scharf
The Hat 6
Spring 2005

About the Money

"When they say it's not about the money, it's about the money."

–Anon.

By the turn of the century
Talking about the money
Replaced talking about the sex,

Talking about one's so-called
Religious life, and all that
Earlier yak about the psyche.

Talking about the money
Got down to it and captured
The hunger, the hope

The love, and the fear:
Let me hear your money talk,
Many sang.

Money was a good time
(What people want most is
Good times and insurance?)

And money picked up
The garbage the following
Morning. (Someone's

Got to do it and someone gets
Money to *do it*.) There was
Really nothing like talking

About the money if you wanted
To really get to know someone,
To get to know what animated,

What moved the American.
Do me. Do it to me, honey.
Do my money. Let's get cynical:

Let me hear your money talk.

Liam Rector
The American Poetry Review
September/October 2005

You Miss It

It's less lonely than it used to be,
what with the forests stripped down
to the minimum now, and the white lines
painted on the Oakwood Mall lot

and the cars parked like brothers,
in order of their arrival,
the sheen of the Lord upon them,
however, the last as blessed
with brightness as the first.

It's less lonely without the animals
broadcasting their strange sense
of themselves, as if being were enough,
if you sang it incessantly
from a high enough branch,
or possibly barked it into the night.

It's less lonely without the barking,
or the baying, or the night itself,
the small eyes clicking off and on
from the brambles, the lit green eyes,
the yellow. Though you miss it,
the loneliness, the size of it mostly,

the way you rose up to meet it
in fear, and were enlarged,
somehow, by the rising
and your own fumbling for sounds,
sequences, syllables

to cast yourself like a spell
into the midst of something
you neither made, nor imagined,
nor could keep from imagining.

Max Garland
The Georgia Review
Volume LIX, Number 1
Spring 2005

The Pier Aspiring

See if you can see how far out it goes; see? You can't see the end!
I'd take you out there
but it's a six hour walk
and the work redundant: one board laid down after another.
When the sun is high
the boards are hot.
Splinters always pose a problem walking any other way but straight.
What keeps me working on it, driving piles,
hauling timber, what's kept my hand
on the hammer, the barnacle scraper,
what keeps me working through the thirst,
the nights when the waves' tops pound
the pier from beneath, what keeps me glad
for the work, the theory is, despite the ridicule
at the lumberyard, the treks with pails
of nails (my arms
2cm longer each trip), the theory
is this: it's my body's habit,
hand over foot, pay check to pay check,
it's in the grain of my bones,
lunch box to lunch bucket.
It's good to wear an X
on my back, to bend my back to the sky, it's right
to use the hammer and the saw,
it's good to sleep
out there – attached at one distant end
and tomorrow adding to that distance.
The theory
is: It will be a bridge.

Thomas Lux
Five Points
Volume 9, Number 2

Suddenly

The truck came at me,
I swerved
but I got a dent.

The car insurance woman
informs me that my policy
has been cancelled.

I say, "You can't do that."
She gives me a little smile
and goes back to her nails.

Lately have you noticed
how aggressively people drive?
A *whoosh!* and whatever.

Some people are suddenly
very rich, and as many
suddenly very poor.

As for the war, don't get me started.
We were too busy watching
the ball game to see

that the things we care about
are suddenly disappearing,
and that they always were.

Louis Simpson
The New Criterion
November 2005

Nothing's As It Should Be

The pie is not easy.
The pin is not neat.
The bees are not busy.
The milk is not meek.

The hound, not lazy.
The clams aren't happy.
The loon is not crazy.
The friend-in-need, snappish.

The cat piss is not mean.
The thieves are not thick.
The hound's tooth is not clean.
The winks are not quick.

The fiddle is not fit.
The bells, never clear.
The honey's never sweet.
The three-dollar bill, unqueer.

The molasses isn't slow.
The church mouse, not poor.
The mule, not stubborn in toto.
The ceiling's not another's floor.

The bunny isn't dumb.
The toothache doesn't hurt.
The rail is not thinsome.
The soil's not cheap as dirt.

The grass isn't green.
The horses aren't healthy.
Nothing's right about the rain:
God's not in Heaven, all's not OK.

Robert Phillips
Chautauqua Literary Journal
Issue 2 – 2005

On Broadway

The planes in the sky still half-empty as ticket sales

plummet. At curtain call, Hedda Gabler dusted off
the gunpowder from her petticoats before thanking us

for coming, a show still in previews, uncertain if

the house would be empty or full come opening night,
the Emmys postponed though Access Hollywood's

back on the air. The St. Petersburg Chamber Orchestra

trying to rebook, eager to risk their lives in order to
perform Rachmaninov's "Vespers." So much rehearsal

wasted. So many bodies to recover. What was to be

must settle for what is – the Towers renamed "the Pile" –
Hedda Gabler better off dead than allowed to play

in boredom – a sure-fire ending staged night after night.

Timothy Liu
For Dust Thou Art
Southern Illinois University Press

When the Watchman Saw the Light

Winter and summer the watchman sat on the roof
of the palace of the sons of Atreus and looked out. Now he tells
the joyful news. He saw a fire flare in the distance.
And he is glad, and his labor is over as well.
It is hard work night and day,
in heat or cold, to look far off
to Arachnaion for a fire. Now the desired
omen has appeared. When happiness
arrives it brings a lesser joy
than expected. Clearly,
we've gained this much: we are saved from hopes
and expectations. Many things will happen
to the Atreus dynasty. One doesn't have to be wise
to surmise this now that the watchman
has seen the light. So, no exaggeration.
The light is good, and those that will come are good.
Their words and deeds are also good.
And we hope all will go well. But
Argos can manage without the Atreus family.
Great houses are not eternal.
Of course, many will have much to say.
We'll listen. But we won't be fooled
by the Indispensable, the Only, the Great.
Some other indispensable, only, and great
is always instantly found.

[1900]

C. P. Cavafy
Translated by Aliki Barnstone
The Collected Poems of C. P. Cavafy
W. W. Norton & Company

NOTE:

Written 1900, unpublished.

The poem is taken from the prologue of Aeschylus's *Agamemnon* (458 B.C.E.), the first play of the *Oresteia* trilogy. King Atreus is the father of Agamemnon and Menelaus. The watchman sees the symbolic fire on Mount Arachnaion, which signifies the end of the Trojan War and Agamemnon's return. Upon his homecoming, he will be murdered by his wife Clytemnestra for having sacrificed their daughter, Iphigenia, to the goddess Artemis. The omen of the light also signals the next tragedy that will befall the cursed House of Atreus.

Our Generation

Whatever they'll say about our delinquencies,
They'll have to agree we managed to bridge the gap
Between those who arrived before us
And those who followed. We learned enough
At the schools available to fill the entry-level positions
At the extant sawmills our elders managed,
At banks, drug stores, freight yards, and hospitals,
Then worked our way up to positions of trust.
There we were, down on the shop floor
Or up in the manager's office, or outside the office
On scaffolds, washing the windows.
Did we work with joy? With no less joy
Than people felt in the generations before us.
And on weekends and weekday evenings
We did our best to pursue the happiness
Our founders encouraged us to pursue,
And with equal gusto. Whatever they say about us
They can't deny that we filled the concert halls,
Movie houses, malls, and late-night restaurants.
We took our bows on stage or waited on tables
Or manned the refreshment booths to earn a little extra
For the things we wanted, the very things
Pursued by the generations before us
And likely to be pursued by generations to come:
Children and lawns and cars and beach towels.
And now and then we stood back to admire
The colorful spectacle, the endless variety,
As others before us admired it, and then returned
To fill our picnic baskets, drive to the park,
And use the baseball diamonds just as their contrivers
Intended they should be used. And if we too
Crowded into the squares to cheer the officials
Who proclaimed our country as fine in fact
As it is in theory, as faithful a friend to the planet
As any country we cared to name,

A few of us confined to a side street,
Carried signs declaring a truth less fanciful.
A few unheeded, to be sure, but no more unheeded
Than a similar few in generations before us
Who hoped that the truth in generations to come,
Though just as homely, would find more followers.

Carl Dennis
The Kenyon Review
New Series, Volume XXVII Number 2
Spring 2005

[I want to build]

I want to build

and raise new
the temples of Theseus and the stadiums
and where Perikles lived

But there's no money, too much spent
today, I had a guest
over   and we sat together

Friedrich Hölderlin
Translated from the German by Richard Sieburth
jubilat
Number 11

Hephaistos

'Hephaistos the renowned smith . . .'
 – the *Iliad*

A man of few words and little grace,
Peter Carey, bachelor, pensioner,
village farrier. As a child
I'd see him Sunday mornings
awkward in an ill-fitting suit
hobbling home from early Mass.
And when I was eight or nine he died.

So, imagine my surprise to meet him now,
this afternoon in the county library,
to find him translated
between the covers of the *Iliad*
conversing with the Immortals:
deity of the dragging footsteps,
old artificer, fire-god,
Hephaistos.

Liam Aungier
Poetry Ireland Review
Issue 84

Icarus Descending

I ride my bicycle to work, leaving earlier than usual
so I can go slow. Everything looks normal,
the air is fresh, the copper
beech trees and the ginkgoes
lush in their end-of-summer foliage,
the street clean from last night's rain.
The men from Public Works
have been here lately and patched a few holes.
Somebody must have complained,
but it wasn't me. The only blemish
on my contentment is the strange sensation
that somebody very like me is falling through the air
right now, close behind me,
from a great height falling – having leapt, or been pushed –
but anyhow no longer cradling his despair,
making light of it, arms outstretched,
though his corduroy sleeves cannot undulate
like feathered wings in figure eights
and he is dropping. How foolish to try
to see him. I don't even twist to look,
the way a dream just after you have woken
has no words for you.

Carol Edelstein
The Disappearing Letters
Perugia Press

Noah at Dusk

Horizon by horizon, the sea had dropped,
and dolphins, quick stitches riding folds of brill,
proved the world could end again; he'd seen, remember,
giraffes' heads bobbing on the swells like flowers

and the last mountain, turned slick last stone,
pitch off its goats. By now the mice, dynastic sailors,
were roistering next to pooled stubs of candle
and the last handfuls of corn. Soon the future would frill

each beak, and his wife, still mucking out stalls
though the others were pressed into portholes
like designs into buttons, would rainbow above him again

as he's hungered a month for her to do. Then this too
would be lost, like the silence just after the rain stops
when all views seem empty, all balance true.

Terri Witek
Image
Art • Faith • Mystery
Number #46
Summer 2005

The Shout

We went out
into the school yard together, me and the boy
whose name and face

I don't remember. We were testing the range
of the human voice:
he had to shout for all he was worth,

I had to raise an arm
from across the divide to signal back
that the sound had carried.

He called from over the park – I lifted an arm.
Out of bounds,
he yelled from the end of the road,

from the foot of the hill,
from beyond the look-out post of Fretwell's Farm –
I lifted an arm.

He left town, went on to be twenty years dead
with a gunshot hole
in the roof of his mouth, in Western Australia.

Boy with the name and face I don't remember,
you can stop shouting now, I can still hear you.

Simon Armitage
The Shout: Selected Poems
Harcourt, Inc.

The Population

One of the feelings which returns so often:
I mean the way that winter afternoons

call back those childhood sulks at the window.
That incessant need to sketch in the people

behind the lichened shingle of facing houses.
Now, when evening gathers, the walls conceal

no lion tamers lounging with the lions,
no divers plunging inside an aquarium.

Just a catch in the stomach like falling:
sweet emptiness . . . which others must also feel.

Even hours after, mothers and children
crossing the bright street by the supermarket

cut such vivid profiles. And they have a fierceness:
like ravenous hummingbirds who couldn't care

about the thorns they thrust through to devour
the little beads of honey in the flower.

Or like themselves . . . Lucent apartments shelve
into the hills, the whole volume of sky

falls on the spaces between, and passing strangers
move with the urgency that darkness

lends them: their skins much brighter against the expanse
of towers, suburbs, and fields they pull behind.

Peter Campion
Other People
The University of Chicago Press

The View from Zero Bridge

My father made his way to Zero Bridge
Before the sun slipped up the riverbed
And lighted plum groves – long before the cars,
Carts, rickshaws, trucks, and bicycles emerged,
Dew-slick at dawn, into the dust. He passed
Our shuttered shop, passed Ram Bagh Road, arrived
And, with his camera, peered over the edge
On long *shikaras* jostling side by side,
Their pointed noses wedged on the stone slab,
Their open bellies full – kohlrabi, beets,
Red carrots, long green *kuddu*, string beans – rows
Piled patchwork, high as each small boat could hold.
The farmers, barefoot, balanced at the edges,
Haggling, counting, weighing. He framed and shot

A young man in an orange cabled sweater
Swinging a bale of okra to his shoulder;
A pyramid of eggplants on a scale;
A farmer setting weights to balance them,
The wind across the Jhelum billowing
His gray pajama. After the shutter closed,
The farmers tipped their heart-shaped paddles, turned,
And rowed to Dal Lake's maze of floating gardens.

It must have been our last year. Had he known,
He would have waited for the shot he missed:
The empty boats, the paddles poised to break
Morning's gold film, laid thin across the lake.

Lynn Aarti Chandhok
The Missouri Review
Volume 28, Number 3
Winter 2005

Subway Seethe

What could have been the big to-do
that caused him to push me aside
on that platform? Was a woman who knew
there must be some good even inside
an ass like him on board that train?
Charity? Frances? His last chance
in a ratty string of last chances? Jane?
Surely in all of us is some good.
Better love thy neighbor, buddy,
lest she shove *back*. Maybe I should.
It's probably just a cruddy
downtown interview leading to
some cheap-tie, careerist, dull
cul-de-sac he's speeding to.
Can he catch up with his soul?
Really, what was the freaking crisis?
Did he need to know before me
if the lights searching the crowd's eyes
were those of our train, or maybe
the train of who he might have been,
the person his own-heart-numbing,
me-shoving anxiety about being
prevents him from ever becoming?
How has his thoughtlessness defiled
who I was before he shoved me?
How might I be smiling now if he'd smiled,
hanging back, as though he might have loved me?

J. Allyn Rosser
Poetry
Volume CLXXXVI, Number 1
April 2005

Selling Out

I

We contracted to sell the lot.
The angle of attack of heavy rain.
The bedroom with the rising damp spot.
The dawn shunt of a gypsum train.
The night creak of boards, metallic pings.
The tree fungi like heaped-up plates.
The valedictory spider tying strings.
Swivel press. Clothesline. Blackbirds in spate.

II

When the sparrow tilted the balance of the pear tree.
When the apples were setting out their stalls.
When the scaly sea sparkled like a fizzy drink.
When the yew thirsted for the juices of the moon.
When your lavender deck chair sprawled
near the gangly hollyhocks.
When the palm tree – so alienated all winter –
fanned itself against premeditated heat.
When the robin came within two feet of your wellingtons.
When the neighbours were away.
When stamens bowed with gold dust.
When rust had yet to blight the lilacs.
When the white of the indecisive butterfly
was like the surface on a bowl of double cream.
When you returned upstairs
and stole a last glance at the view.
When you found the sky had misted over.
When the deed was done.

Dennis O'Driscoll
New and Selected Poems
Anvil Press Poetry

Chess Match Ends in Fight

As one opponent calling out checkmate
an hour past midnight could crack a man

already broken and bring allegations
from his tongue, violence to his veins,

bring him to rise and hip-knock the table
so the legs screech, so the pieces quiver

and topple, the bishop a salt shaker
kissed by an elbow, bring him to blows,

to blows, to blows, to grasp the winner
and propel him through plate glass

as if a baptism in geometric water,
so the glass rains and dazzles the floor,

so he emerges from the window stunned,
lacerated, to bring blood and the lilac

breath of night, men with stars pinned
to their chests, handcuffs jingling,

so one's booked, the other's stitched,
the coarse thread lacing up the lesions,

as and so and to bring this to this,
we will be there with our brooms.

David Hernandez
Always Danger
Southern Illinois University Press

Kitty Oppenheimer Tends Louis Slotin after an Accident in the Lab

I hadn't seen Hiroshima myself,
or Nagasaki, though I'd heard Bob Serber's
stories. They seemed like fairy tales or myths –
fables to frighten children, or at best
efforts to cast the inexplicable
in human terms. But then I tended Slotin
his last nine days and saw. Saw him vomit
till his stomach bled. Saw him try to grip
the white enamel bowl in the crotches of his thumbs,
his hands so swollen that his fingers wouldn't bend.
Saw him retch clear strands of spit, green flecks
of bile, too tired to wipe them from his lips.
He hiccuped for ten hours straight. At first
he almost laughed; later we strapped him down
to stop him clawing at his diaphragm.
Blisters grew like toadstools on his hands,
between his fingers, up his arms. The skin
peeled off his chest. His hair came out in clumps.
His liver failed. His kidneys. Bowels blocked.
Blood filled the bedpans. We gave him codeine.
Morphine. Nothing helped. Pain paced his body.
His fingers and his toes turned blue. His face
bloated, blistered, thick as a mask. A rind.
He seemed unconscious – so we had to think.
He might have been a thousand different men.
A hundred thousand. Only, when he died,
no cities burned. Friends grieved. His parents took
a lead-lined coffin back to Winnipeg.

John Canaday
The Cincinnati Review
Volume 2, Number 2
Winter 2005

from "Natural History"
The Bear

In quiet, in the exquisite privacy of a cave, a bear
      gives birth. Outside the cave it's rain, a driving rain,

but inside there is no sound, only the thump-thump
      of her convulsing body and her babies' cries.

Her cubs are white screaming lumps, eyeless until
      she licks their eyes into place, bald until

she paints fur up and down their bodies with her tongue.
      It is a litter of five, at least; it is hard to see

how many have burrowed under her soft belly.
      Also, this is ancient Rome; it is hard to see through

so much time. It makes you wonder how many
      other beautiful sights are hidden away in time,

a cavelike element noted for its dimness. Now she
      and her cubs are emerging from the cave, leaving

one weakling behind. He is lame, and will not survive
      this rainy night two thousand years ago. By now

he is vanishing into the floor of the dark cave,
      even his newly painted fur, even his fresh eyes.

By now he's gone entirely from view.
      All the caves on this hill are identical again.

Dan Chiasson
Natural History
Alfred A. Knopf

Who the Meek Are Not

Not the bristle-bearded Igors bent
under burlap sacks, not peasants knee-deep
    in the rice paddy muck,
nor the serfs whose quarter-moon sickles
    make the wheat fall in waves
they don't get to eat. My friend the Franciscan
    nun says we misread
that word *meek* in the Bible verse that blesses them.
    To understand the meek
(she says) picture a great stallion at full gallop
    in a meadow, who –
at his master's voice – seizes up to a stunned
    but instant halt.
So with the strain of holding that great power
    in check, the muscles
along the arched neck keep eddying,
    and only the velvet ears
prick forward, awaiting the next order.

Mary Karr
Sinners Welcome
HarperCollins*Publishers*

The Private Meditations of John Wyclif: On Angels

By now no one cares how many would fit on the head of a pin.
They can always make themselves smaller, or the pin bigger,
and being infinite they have all infinity to play scholastic
games. Meanwhile, they watch us in our lecture hall
and see that our only way to fit another scholar in
is by one of us dying. To this the angels have
only pity. They turn the pin on its head,
and then as many angels as the last
scholar has conjectured climb
up the side. They reach
the tip and dance in
bare feet to bleed
for us. This,
we see,
was al-
ways
the
po-
in
t.

Thom Satterlee
Image
Art • Faith • Mystery
Number #47
Fall 2005

Far Niente

Nothing's far
Beyond our ken.
Anything's nearer;
And something everyone

Can head for, fast and
Furious. But just to the stone men
(Near the end of the fever)
Takes the most curious

Almost forever.
And nothing is farther again.
Nothing is nearer the truth.
So it was
At the first–we were wholly immersed–then

We burst into youth . . .

Heather McHugh
TriQuarterly 120

Elegance

All that is uncared for.
Left alone in the stillness
in that pure silence married
to the stillness of nature.
A door off its hinges,
shade and shadows in an empty room.
Leaks for light. Raw where
the tin roof rusted through.
The rustle of weeds in their
different kinds of air in the mornings,
year after year.
A pecan tree, and the house
made out of mud bricks. Accurate
and unexpected beauty, rattling
and singing. If not to the sun,
then to nothing and to no one.

Linda Gregg
In the Middle Distance
Graywolf Press

Description of a Lost Thing

It never had a name,
Nor do I remember how I found it.
I carried it in my pocket
Like a lost button
Except it wasn't a button.

Horror movies,
All-night cafeterias,
Dark barrooms
And poolhalls,
On rain-slicked streets.

It led a quiet, unremarkable existence
Like a shadow in a dream,
An angel on a pin,
And then it vanished.
The years passed with their row

Of nameless stations,
Till somebody told me *this is it!*
And fool that I was,
I got off on an empty platform
With no town in sight.

Charles Simic
My Noiseless Entourage
Harcourt, Inc.

They Had Torn Off My Face at the Office

They had torn off my face at the office.
The night that I finally noticed
that it was not growing back, I decided
to slit my wrists. Nothing ran out;
I was empty. Both of my hands fell off
shortly thereafter. Now at my job
they allow me to type with the stumps.
It pleases them to have helped me,
and I gain in speed and confidence.

Ted Kooser
Flying at Night: Poems 1965-1985
University of Pittsburgh Press

Empty similes

Like standing in front of a woman who says thank you
when you tell her you love her, that stuck

sound of a crow, pulling the one nail from its voice
outside your window and you

going down to the sea too late, where it was
three million years ago, waving your little towel
at the shadow of waves, like dropping

your stomach when you drop the phone,
a voice spinning at the end of the chord, your mother,
father, everyone

dead, even the person telling you
gone and you
waving your metronome arm, and time

inside the trees making clocks we check
by cutting them down.

Bob Hicok
The Iowa Review
Volume 35, Number 3
Winter 2005/06

My First Mermaid

I

In Florida, where these things can happen,
we stopped at the last roadside attraction.

Into a small theater decorated with mold,
we descended. Behind a curtain sagging like seaweed,

a wall of glass held back a wall of water.
And there in the springs, a woman wearing bikini top

and Lycra fish tail held an air hose to her lips
like a microphone. What was she waiting for?

Into the great open bowl of the springs,
a few fish drifted. They looked at the two of us.

They shook their heads and their whole bodies rippled.
Air bubbles shimmered in the filtered Florida sun,

each a silver O racing to the surface to break.
We'd missed the day an unscripted underwater blimp

of a manatee wobbled into view. The gray, whiskered lard
of a sea cow or the young woman who sang –

lip-synched, rather – some forgettable song,
her lipstick waterproof: which was the real mermaid?

II

Given the weight of water, nothing happens fast
to a mermaid, whether it's love or loss.

Not like the landlocked life, I wanted to warn her.
But here came a prince in street clothes,

trying to think thoughts that were heavy enough
to make himself sink to her level. His shirt ballooned,

a man made not into merman but to manatee.
Yet, in the small eternity it took for him

to grasp her slippery flipper, for her to find
his more awkward human ankle, and then

for them to turn, head over each other's heels –
a ring rolling away too beautifully to catch –

they lived happily ever after.
Until one of them had to stop for breath.

Debora Greger
The Kenyon Review
New Series, Volume XXVII Number 4
Fall 2005

Two Children Threatened by a Nightingale

Attentive as one is to a whisper, the children wade through standing water, uncertain of its depth or source. They find and salvage a sogged train schedule. For their short lives the depot has been boarded shut. One has a flair for death and can fashion a noose from corn silk. One keeps an archive of diaries. One is the movie extra a camera seeks out, lingers on. One reads the subtitles aloud before the characters speak. One imagines sleep to be a furnished room. One imagines rain on the rolled hay, the must of empty stables, the tin-edge of blood on the tongue. By schema and classifications, they are a sister and a brother. Waylaid between this puddle and the next, one creates a theory of the spectral. One fingers through a cache of candies. One is plump and ready for the oven. One could not even flavor a stock pot. One is the overlooked subject. One is a language of mishearings. They cling to the hitherto unknown. When they dissect the bird they find nothing of the song.

Eric Pankey
Bat City Review
Number 1
Spring/Summer 2005

Two Wheeler Spins

She wakes up and she's a bicycle.
Streamline, at last.
Bicycles are naturally anorexic.
Sometimes her husband pats her seat.
Sex is not out of the question.
They're not a run of the mill couple.

She wakes up and she's a rowboat,
sturdy in the water.
The couple she carries
are her parents, red-faced
and exhausted after sex.
She drifts in silence,
heavy with their regret.

Or she wakes up and she's a door
leaning against the bicycle
she once was, or a boat.
How to keep her husband
alert in these scenes?

He pulls out a key.
They're face to face
remembering excursions.
Inside their rooms, the parents
live quietly in picture frames.

Colette Inez
Pleiades
Volume 25 Number 2, 2005

The Fire Museum

Beside the copper bell and hammer,
a tea-brown gas mask stares out, left eye
cracked. A tangle of rope, blackened
and frayed, lies pressed under glass
like a lock of hair. What doesn't burn
becomes relic, talisman against.

On a scroll, huge petals of fire curl
from a wooden house. Firemen run
bare-legged toward it, tattooed
with the motifs of invulnerability:
twisting carp, samurai, a red octopus
winding around the back and arms.

Their bodies glow on the paper
like the painted lanterns they carry
running, themselves lit.

Jennifer Fumiko Cahill
Gulf Coast
Spring/Fall 2005

House Guest

Nor is the prophet Elijah the only one to put on the garb of a beggar.
The Angel of Death delights in frightening men in the same way.

—*Elie Wiesel*, Dawn

When he comes to your door, you cannot risk refusal.
You offer warm, crusted breads, hollow and lightly sanded
as coffins; alphabet soup with solar flares of carrots,
penumbras of barley. You were not, you explain,

prepared for a guest. When he lifts the bowl to drink broth,
you try to believe he is not reading and then swallowing
your name. What else can you give as hospitable distraction?
Coffee in a bone china cup? You remind yourself he's come

as a beggar, not a chic reviewer, though by Sunday, you offer
trowel wedges of cucumber sandwich, set his glass on thin
cork. You begin to remember deaths, brief and out of context

as postcards: a burro you once saw fight itself dead, trapped
half out of its mother; a neighbor's cat which ate her own kittens;
your grandmother, drugged in a pink bathrobe. You suspect
that *you* are the beggar – your tin cup of graciousness

empty. And though you say nothing, you find him next morning
making waffles from scratch. He fills their square pillows
with syrup and brews you Earl Grey. In the bathroom, he's left
new soaps wrapped in tissue paper like a nice hotel, washcloths

folded like flowers. You pretend such luxury is natural – each day
more fearfully accustomed to the wings brushing your arm;
you read the paper silently together: first comics, then obits, then news.

Alexandra Teague
Crazyhorse
Number 67
Spring 2005

Ghazal: Waiting

What follows when imagination's not inspired by waiting,
body and spirit rendered sick and tired by waiting?

Wrinkles, stock market losses, abscessed teeth, rejection slips:
some of the benefits acquired by waiting.

Taught from childhood that patience is a virtue,
she thought that she could get what she desired by waiting.

History, a child at the chapter's cusp
can only find out what transpired by waiting.

Does anyone escape alienated labor's
cycle of being hired, exploited, made redundant, fired, by waiting?

He rolls a pen like a chess-piece between thumb and forefinger:
he won't emerge from the morass in which he's mired by waiting.

If poetry's imagination's daughter,
didn't someone say that she was sired by waiting?

She raised her children, wrote at dawn, ignored the factions,
arrived at being read, remembered and admired by waiting.

Once a pair of lovers downed shots in a Chelsea bar.
their nerves and fantasies hot-wired by waiting.

Sweating, shackled and blindfolded in a basement,
will I get out, the hostage (of whom) inquired, by waiting?

Marilyn Hacker
Virginia Quarterly Review
Volume 82, Number 1
Winter 2006

Enemies of Enormity

And thanks to a polymer the chemists jimmied-up in Bern
she can sweep a thin streak of blush across her cheeks
as any young woman might
if the spring is passing
as it is passing
through the well-advertised & transnational influence
of Chanel's "instant radiance to go" –
this skin of hers
a little skanky she almost thinks to herself
while staring in the mirror –
tho for this working girl & everyone else alive
today is a Tuesday a May 27th that no one can make behave
so that at the same time the girl is worrying her makeup
across the street in front of the post office
a panhandler in shorts is taking off his leg,
his plastic prosthesis unstrapped at the knee
its buckles bent & chafing, he holds his free hand cupped for coins
while the other rubs at the stump, absentmindedly stroking it
the way a man might the belly of his wife
if she were just three or four months pregnant,
that is to say, lightly,
his eyes inflected by worries, slight misgivings, fears,
but whose wouldn't be?
who wouldn't be afraid that the leg might be stolen?
it could happen, you might be distracted by a passing bus –
on the side of the bus a pin dropping in midair –
the pin imprinted there on the poster
the same pin
so often caught in the act of falling on a television screen
but in slow motion
as it bounces on a glass table
by the mouthpiece of a white telephone
clarity is what's at stake it's said, who we are –
a light tap when the pin hits the glass –
and even if no one is sure that what they've heard
is what they were supposed to hear,
exultant or glamorous, precarious or sad,
they will all go ahead with what they have planned

for themselves
if only
it could be a moment when they stand unburdened
before this evening's bloody meats
tomorrow's thunderclap.

David Rivard
Sugartown
Graywolf Press

I Followed a Ribbon

I followed a ribbon that trailed from a hand
and it led through the grazing of crowds upon pavement,
through laities and simpering voices in evening,
past lives that might be given me in confidence
and confidences that cannot be given in life,
through the drawers of perished infants, where the bed
linens still keep the traces of tiny bodies,
and beside ladders upon which men stand
as on a willful pride that harms all those beneath,
all down, all down at last, to the harbor
where such ribbons trail the water in a hundred places.
I cannot find my own amidst so many,
but I pretend to, and taking up an oar I leap
foolhardy into a passing boat.
"Do you need an oarsman?" I call out needlessly.
As if there were anything left to do but row.

Jesse Ball
The Paris Review
Number 174
Summer 2005

Resistance

We retreated to the forests
and from the forests
to the mountains.

We were not lost,
and we could not be
found. Expecting nothing,

we followed no strategy.
We were not concerned
with innocence

and guilt, ignored the conscription
of symbols. We learned
to accept the presence

of initial conditions.
The movement meant nothing
to us; the sanctification

of resistance
was unknown.
The instrument of violence

was something
we borrowed and returned
when we were done.

They expected our resistance
to weaken and disappear,
but, like desire,

it was not something
we could dispense
with. Sharing everything,

we were never alone.
Like a choir,
we blended together,

retreating to the forests
and from the forests
to the mountains.

Peter Leight
AGNI 62

Miss Congeniality

There's a name given
after your death
and a name you must answer to while you're alive.

Like flowers, my friends – nodding, nodding. My
enemies, like space, drifting
away. They

praised my face, my enunciation, and the power
I freely relinquished, and the fires
burning in the basements

of my churches,
and the pendulums swinging
above my towers.
And my

heart (which was a Boy Scout

lost for years in a forest). And my

soul (although the judges said
it weighed almost nothing
for goodness had devoured it).

They praised my feet, the shoes
on my feet, my feet
on the floor, the floor –
and then

the sense of despair
I evoked with my smile, the song

I sang. The speech
I gave
about peace, in praise of the war. O,

they could not grant me the title I wanted

so they gave me the title I bore,

and stubbornly refused
to believe I was dead
long after my bloody mattress

had washed up on the shore.

Laura Kasischke
New England Review
Volume 26, Number 4 / 2005

Pain Tries to Think of Something

Ties a string around one finger.
Places a stone in each shoe. Stuffs
its clothes with paper,

watches sleeves catch and smoke.
Rubs its knees together, feeling
nerves flare. Tries to think

of literature physics shopping
malls lighted all night cups
of milk it exhorts its children

to drink every morning combing
their hair and attaching each
neckline's bitten hook and eye.

The children finish their juice
and cereal and try to guess
what animal what shape what color

is next while Pain weeps,
imagining an elephant hiding its bird-
like face in the trees.

At night while the children
sleep Pain thinks of the last thing,
watching the moon-

monument rise, then thinks
of something else, the body's mud
and straw crouched beneath stars.

Laurie Lamon
The Fork Without Hunger
CavanKerry Press

Dress Rehearsal

His second act costume weighs fifteen pounds,
and he must dance in it under hot lights
while singing with an alto whose voice sounds
like a full moon blazing on summer nights.

Smiling all the while, he must project ease,
the wit of a rogue prince whose true passion
is for battle, and grace enough to please
this young partner. But his face is ashen,

brow drenched. Breath is elusive as the birds
he tries to describe in this endless song.
He stops. If he could recall the rhymed words
that take him offstage now, he would be gone

for good. Nothing comes to him. There are wings
everywhere, action shattering the still
moment he hoped to create. Hazy rings
of light, behind which an audience will

be applauding at this time tomorrow,
fade as he awaits the falling curtain
now, lost in a soft, rapturous sorrow
where nothing moves and nothing is certain.

Floyd Skloot
The Hudson Review
Volume LVIII, Number 2
Summer 2005

Six at the Beginning

means:
When ribbon grass is pulled up, the sod comes with it.
–I Ching

You know this one. He's old.
And rich. He can do what he
wants. It would even be boring,
but there's a threat to the soil.
She has the naked glance of
fourteen, hair tucked beneath

her cap, and he wants to take
that, the lustrous unveiling.
It's hard to be without the cash
to crush a fat old man, hard to
face it, as you julienne the carrots
in his wife's kitchen. She stands

with a knife in her hand as he
comes downstairs. The curls fall
like ribbons, filling the hollow
at her neck. And though we
want to say at the end that she
recovers wholly, it isn't true.

Deborah Bogen
The Gettysburg Review
Volume 19, Number 1
Spring 2006

talking at blerancourt

wed just driven down on a grey december day from
a conference on recent american poetry that jacques darras
had organized at his university in amiens where most of the
talks were by french scholars and poets   but hed also
brought over a bunch of american poets and arranged a
reading for us at the the museum of french american
cooperation at blerancourt   an old estate that once
belonged to j.p. morgan and had been turned over to the french
government some time after the first world war   whose
battles had left shell scars on the walls of the older buildings
        there were six of us poets who were going to read and
we were joined by serge faucherau   a well known french
critic translator and anthologist of american poetry who was
going to produce part of the introduction along with jacques
        so with only about twenty minutes of time available i
figured id read a couple of short written pieces because it
was not the time or place for a talk poem
        jackson maclow and jerry rothenberg had just read and
then it was my turn   but jacques introduced me as a talk
poet   they were all expecting a talk poem   so what could i
do
        with all the others i had walked in the cold december rain
over the weirdly topiaried gardens that reminded me of alain
resnais' "last year at marienbad"   id examined the strange
collection of paintings   mostly by minor american painters
whod happened to spend time in france   id seen the dark green
first world war ambulance displayed like a found object in one of
the halls   id read the walt whitman poem to france on the
occasion of the franco prussian war that was displayed in
manuscript in one of the glass cases and i figured   ill do the
best i can

someone asked me once   a simple question   an absurdly
simple question   and i gave an absurdly simple answer   whats an
artist he asked and i said somebody who does the best he can
        by now ive said this so many times ive begun to believe it
    because when you think about it there are very few people in this
world that do the best they can

you know   if general motors makes

a lemon of a car its your problem   but if an artist makes a lousy

artwork its his problem or her problem   so it turns out that artists are the last

people in this world who have to do the best they

can   because their life is at stake

you say you know a plumber who does the best he can   i say hes an

artist   you know lots of artists who dont do the best they

can?   its very simple   theyre not artists   anyhow   thats

how i answer the question   because up to now thats the best i can do for an

answer

now as a poet   thats the term i get stuck with

i actually choose

it   fairly aggressively   i choose it in spite of the fact that i tend

to feel a little uncomfortable with it   because if im going to be a

poet i want to be a poet who explores mind as the medium of his

poetry   not mind as a static thing   but the act of thinking   and

the closest i can come to the act of thinking is the act of talking and

thinking at the same time   the closest I can come to my thinking is

by talking myself through it   talking my way through my thinking

thinking my way through my talking

a little while ago jacques asked do we have the right material here

and maybe he was talking about the tape recorder   but

thinking about it in general   i suppose theres no such thing as the

wrong material   were in a museum here   a small museum of

french american friendship and museums have a strange effect on me

and this museum   like any museum

but in this museum even more

so   because its a small museum

looking at the pictures on the

walls   theres something arbitrary about a museums relation to

artists   a little like looking at driftwood on a beach   the

artists are cast up on the shore after the ship has gone down

and theyre carried some distance by the current and stranded on this

particular beach   where they get found and hung on the wall

trophies of a random rescue

museums do the best they can   and i suppose i repeat myself but my

sense is that museums are to artists as anthologies are to

poets as zoos are to animals   and its hard to think about animals in a zoo

where the animals are sleeping while the people are buying

ice cream and t-shirts and toys   its even hard to look at artworks in some

galleries   but i got used to it because i had to act as an art

critic which ive done for a large part of my life   and i had to find a

way to do that and live with being an artist   a poet   at the same
time
         now the way that i managed to do it was to speak as one artist to another
and anyone else who cared to listen   so if anyone
     wanted to eavesdrop they could   but i wasnt writing for them
         and if they didnt want to listen it was all right with me   but
what i had to say seemed to amuse a lot of people   and the
magazines printed it even though i was lousy about deadlines   and at
one point i was told by donald droll   a friend of mine who ran the
     fischback gallery   that a german magazine with a remarkable name
das kunstwerk   wanted to talk with me about becoming their
american correspondent and write about the art scene in new york
         id already been writing a new york chronicle for a danish magazine
called *billedkunst*   so i said okay donald what are they interested in
         donald said the editors are coming to town next week   theyll
take you to an expensive restaurant and youll find out when you see
     them
         the next week two well-dressed germans appeared at the fischback
gallery and they told me all about art   they told me
all sorts of things   and for someone who understands german very
well i didnt know what they were talking about   they were talking
about valuable art   expensive art   mind-boggling art   and
censored art   they wanted me to write about important art
         about art that was winning art that was losing and art that was
important
         look i said i dont know about all that   i go around to galleries
to artists studios to museum shows   i think about what interests
     me and then i write about it   is that all right with you
         they looked disappointed   they thought i would give them
something definitive and i would have liked to give them something
definitive but i didnt know anything definitive   i go into galleries to
     see whats there   and sometimes its all right and sometimes its not
         sometimes im depressed   most of the time its just not
interesting   but dont get me wrong   sometimes there are
wonderful works   its just not often   but i keep going around
     i do the best i can   even though i hadnt developed my definition yet
i did the best i could   and it was one of those years   it was a year
where a great number of my friends were showing things   things i
could think about   it was winter and there was a sculptor   an
englishman   an english sculptor   a charming man   as elegant and
handsome as general wavell or ronald colman   an evasively

intelligent slim and moustached man who was coming to have a show
at the fischback gallery   and the opening was set for a friday in
   february   and i had seen a couple of the works earlier   my
friend donald had shown them to me

they were small moulded plastic
shapes about the size of a large door handle   they were white and shiny little
organic shapes   and if you picked them up they looked
   back at you blankly   throwing back at you a dim reflection of your face
they were constantly rejecting   they had a kind of enigmatic fascination in their
refusal small as they were to be loveable

thats the way they looked in the back room   because thats
where you see a lot of the art before its lit and set on the stage when
   youre a working critic   they take you into the back room before
the lights are up and the orchestra plays   so to speak   because
they hope youll review it before it opens   but thats how theyll show
it to you anyway even if you cant

so i went into the back room and saw these little enigmatic
shapes   and i was waiting to see what they would look like when
   the show finally opened   wondering whether you could still see
your reflection when they were under plexi when the lights hit them

the gallery was planning a big opening   the sculptor had come all the
way from beirut where he was teaching at the american college

and there was a picture of the american college in beirut in the
new york times with a short article about the sculptor the day before the opening
the day of the opening new york had one of the worst
   snowstorms in its history   four people came to the opening   ellie and me
and marilyn fischback and donald droll   and the snow lingered
   and because nobody knew him and nobody could be charmed by him at
the opening   so nobody came to see the show with its snow
   colored little sculptures and it was not reviewed   and the elegant sculptor
went back to the american college in beirut and never
   appeared in new york again

now as an artist he was no worse and he was a lot better than many
artists who appeared again and again   but what was i to write
   in *das kunskwerk*   that these brilliant hard white plastic sculptures
had been caught in a storm that buried them like a deluge of styrofoam
   and the sculptor had disappeared into beirut   would anyone have
cared   could i have written sufficiently eloquently in german for them
   to understand about the pathos and the loss of the show to him   who would
never come back to new york his two years of work gone   or to us who would
have to give up the possibility of finding

meaning in those tough little white shapes   but you know it was like that
new york was filled with excitement and disappointment

    yet thats not what they wanted you to write about   they wanted you to
write about important art   about artists you knew
   would come back to new york again and again   and i was a working
critic and mostly thats what i wrote about   the scene
      and i got started writing for it because an old friend nicco calas
had persuaded me to   he introduced me to lita hornick   so i
started my art writing by taking over the art chronicle from frank
  o'hara for her magazine *kulchur*   and then john ashbery whod
published one of my first art essays in *art and literature* came back
from paris to help edit *art news*   where he persuaded tom hess to
publish more of my essays   so i was very much a part of the new
york art scene from about 1964 on   but after a few years i was
  beginning to get a little tired of it
    so john whod become a good friend and something of a comrade in arms at
art news decided to help me   john decided to help me into
a kind of curatorial career   he knew that jerome robbins wanted to
organize an exhibition for the education and edification of his dancers
and john decided i was the one to do it   so he provided me with an
introduction to robbins

                    like many new york poets I was an aficionado of
dance   so i knew of the man   i knew that robbins imagined
himself as a kind of choreographer diaghilev   diaghilev had
been a formidably cultivated man whod taken it upon himself to educate all of
his disciples of the ballet russe in all of the arts   he
would drag nijinsky and fokine to contemporary painting exhibitions
    to concerts of modern music to poetry readings and in this way he brought
together people like fokine nijinsky massine and karsavina
  and spessivtseva with painters like picasso and braque   poets like
    apollinalre and cocteau and composers like stravinsky satie or ravel
     and robbins wanted to drag his dancers into contemporary art in
the same way   jerome robbins was an american and he was not a
diaghilev   he was a choreographer who wanted to be a diaghalev
but knew he wasnt   so he needed somebody to help him be diaghilev
    so john arranges it and i go to meet jerome robbins   who is a little
imperious man   "what" he asked me as soon as i walked in "do
you think of paul cadmus"   paul cadmus was a perfectly competent
gay painter who specialized in representations of winsome academic
  male nudes   in 1967 he was about as contemporary as tchelitchev
    i told him i never thought of cadmus

so "what kind of show would you put on" he said   and before i could
answer   he said "let me show you my space" and got up to
  lead me there   in fact he didnt get up   he shot up and started walking
from the room   in fact he bolted from the room and he wasnt walking he was
loping   he was moving very quickly in what was almost a half run disguised as
a walk

                                                      now i am not inordinately sensitive to
one-upmanship   but it didnt take much effort for me to realize he
was moving so fast that unless i wanted to join in his masquerade id have to
jog to keep up with him   and i was not about to play his game
  so I set out at a very deliberate pace and ambled into his dance space a good
thirty seconds after him   where i found him seated
  on a high stool from which he snarled at me
    "so what would you show my dancers?"
      now you have to remember this was 1967 or so and most of my friends
were minimalist sculptors   so i suggested i wouldnt show
  them things   i would get artists like robert morris or carl andre or
don judd or ronny bladen or sal romano or walter de maria to confront them with
things   obstacles over and under and around which they would have to work
because i didnt see art then as so much showing
  things as performing   i said i would put on a show for them that didnt look
like art but would be the most interesting art by some of the
  most interesting artists of the time
      now you have to understand that jerome robbins had led me a chase into
his dance space   he had seemed to be walking but had
  actually been running in order to force me to struggle to keep up with
him   and i had realized this   and stubborn person that i am i had
  sauntered after him so that he had to wait nearly thirty seconds for
  me to arrive and he had asked me about paul cadmus and i had
  proposed minimalist sculpture   so in a state of rage he pointed to his pristine
dance floor and demanded "how would you do that"   and
  i answered "right on the dance floor   id get everything else out of here and fill
up the place with all the junk that was needed for your
  dancers to have to dodge skip jump over or be tripped by   so your
dancers could encounter the real world they live in"   this didnt sound
  like diaghilev and needless to say i never did the exhibition
      so you can see i had a real relation to the contemporary art
scene   even if it was equivocal   and i suppose i wrote equivocally about it
sometimes about the people everybody knew and
  sometimes about people very few people knew   and sometimes
about ideas that were going around in it that i wanted to think about

so i wrote a piece called "pop – a few clarifications" for *das
kunstwerk* and they seemed to like it   because they eventually
published it and sent me back a copy of the magazine whose contents
i dont remember   all i remember was its cover   a remarkable
black and white photo of a soho rooftop with three young people
  sitting there   and there was something haunting about this image
of the three of them stranded in this unlikely space   the two
artists and the actress i recognized as delfine seyrig   the incredibly
beautiful star of alan resnais' "last year at Marienbad"   who in robbe
  grillets' script was always stranded between two men and a past and
future she couldnt reconcile
          now mostly what the art magazines want is essays that promote
the importance of whatever is going on at any moment in the art world
  by promoting the artists and exhibitions that galleries and museums happen to
be staging at the time   which is why galleries and
museums advertise there   to create the impression that theyre
  participating in a world in which so much of so much importance is
happening   when in reality very little is usually happening
          and to help give shape to such an impression   museums often
reshuffle the artists and artworks they usually exhibit   or have
seen other museums or galleries exhibit   into theme shows that the
    magazines try to address with "think pieces" that attempt to articulate the
"issues" these shows are supposed to illuminate   now
art news was at that time a serious magazine that   in addition to
  the usual promotional activities conducted by all the art world
publications printed serious essays on art   and tom hess   who
  was its publisher and editor-in-chief   was a sensitive and intelligent art critic
who was close to the artists he admired and had
  recruited his reviewers and essayists from a wide range of
contemporary poets and art historians   and he encouraged me to
  take on one of these theme shows
          it was an expensive and extensive show put on with a large
fanfare by the museum of modern art in new york and it was i suppose
  intended to address the current interest   this was 1968   of
young artists in new technologies   but the museum of modern art
was a historical museum devoted to a particular history of modernism
  and its continuities   so the show was a historical show curated by
a man named pontus hulten   who was something of a stuffed owl
  a scholarly gentleman not too familiar with really contemporary art and much
more comfortable with the interests and art of the early
  twentieth century   so the show turned out to be an exhibition of old

art and old technology and was almost inevitably called "the machine"
while the technology of the second half of the twentieth century
was more about information processing and control and transmission
devices   about computers and masers and lasers   and usually
led to variously high tech sculptural installations that tom   who was
much more committed to the career of serious painting   wasnt
really familiar with or interested in   so he may have overvalued
the show and thought i should do a think piece about it
but for me it was old technology and old art   so how was i to address it
i did it by inventing a machine   which in a fit of modesty i attributed to
jean tinguely   a machine   an information processing
machine i designated as a *self stabilizing data processing device*
the novelty of which was that it was able by means of successive passes
through a series of analyzer banks   garble heads and erase
heads to render all new data submitted to it identical to the data
already in its memory system   what you knew before you know now
and i presented the patent application for *jean tinguelys new*
machine as an introduction to my essay   preceded by a functional
input output diagram of its manner of operation   the form of which
bore an odd resemblance to the ground plan of the old museum of
modern art   but the application was composed in the prose of patent
language   and the resemblance seemed to have slipped by nearly
everyone who read through the accumulation of technological shaggy
dog stories that formed the body of the essay   it slipped by my
good friend tom hess   and harris rosenstein   who edited the
essay   and i suppose believed along with everyone else that there
really was such a tinguely machine that i was simply commenting on
of course tom probably didnt care very much and merely enjoyed the
stories   while harris may have been suspicious   because he
was an all around new york intellectual   the kind that probably doesnt exist
anymore   a rumpled shirtsleeved chainsmoking
dedicated art world professional who would care more about the meaning of a
new rothko painting or a morton feldman composition
than a subway strike or a collapse of the stock market   and knew
the arts as well as most of the writers whose essays he edited
though he never published a word of his own but edited all of us for
years   but he never said a word to me about it at the time
then suddenly *art news* was sold and fell into the hands of idiots
and not long afterward charming gallant tom hess died and the
old *art news* team disbanded   betsy baker went to take over *art*
in america   john ashbery went off to write an art criticism page for

newsweek   and harris rosenstein went off to administer for the
de menil collection in houston
        it was hard to imagine harris and sheila in houston   stranded on the
coast of texas near galveston   in a raw redneck town with a
couple of great museums   a city of flimsy woodframe houses
strung out around a tiny downtown area   where a few tall glass and
steel buildings huddle up against each other like gaunt pioneers seeking
 shelter on a windy plain and overhang a cavernous underground space
filled with chic boutiques and stylish eating places   to which sleekly
dressed men and women from the corporate world of the tall buildings
 come to lunch and browse and shop   but which emptied out by five
oclock leaving nothing behind but dioramas of impeccably tailored
 silent mannequins blindly offering on gracefully outstretched arms to the vacant
corridors the jewelled accessories of a perished dynasty
    seemingly destroyed by something like a neutron bomb
        but visiting houston several years later   there was some
sort of occasion   a conference or symposium of some kind held in
one of the tall downtown buildings   that brought me and my friend
sheldon nodelman to houston that year   and i took the occasion as
 an opportunity to visit the rothko chapel   which id never seen and
the de menil collection   and naturally we went to visit with harris and sheila
to see how they were holding up in houston   and they
 seemed to be holding up pretty well   under the circumstances of
being stranded in houston   harris was handling the publications of
the de menil collection   which included nursing sheldons great book
 on the rothko chapel through an endless series of deepening revisions
and expansions   and sheila   in spite of all odds had turned the de
menil bookstore into a kind of cultural oasis for concerts and readings
    so that nearly everyone who had anything to do with contemporary
art who passed through houston connected with them
        so we had dinner with them   a whole bunch of us went off
with harris and sheila to an improbably distinguished chinese
restaurant in a seedy part of town far from the glass and steel center
 where our hotel was located   and it was a kind of new york occasion
with lots of noisy esthetic arguments   was rothko a colorist even if he denied
it   were his brightly colored paintings intended to be
"beautiful"   how black were the chapel paintings   were they
"beautiful"   what about the recent fashion in performance art
    and were we finally through with technological art   or would it recur as
regularly as the colored leaves of a northeastern autumn   in the midst of
which harris reminded me of my tinguely piece

"you know" he said "the fourth time i read it i realized it was
terribly funny"

the night got later and we descended into the obligatory personal
chronicles   who was sleeping with whom now that whoever was no longer
with whom but with whoever else   and finally sheldon and i
took a taxi back toward our hotel   and as we came out of the
neighborhoods of small houses and two-storey buildings with store
fronts and drove into the central space of the slim tall buildings the
streets   that had been sparsely peopled before   became
completely empty and silent   as though vacated by something like a
neutron bomb   and as we were driving through the narrow canyon
between the glass and steel buildings out comes a small black
barouche about a block ahead of us drawn by a white horse with a
little plume carrying a formally dressed man and woman   it travels another
block turns a corner and disappears   "sheldon   what was
that?"   "what?"   "the black carriage the white horse"   "i didnt
see anything"

a year or two later sheila died of lung cancer   i guess all that
chainsmoking finally got her   and harris was really stranded on the coast of
texas near galveston   but he held together for about
another year   till hed finally nursed sheldons great rothko book
through the press   and then harris also died

David Antin
Fence
Volume 5, Number 2
Fall/Winter 2002-2003

Small parts slowly

Small parts slowly at work   –vivid automata–   a second-hand stammers
        round a clock face   a nervous child
      casting   shadows   as   it   goes   round   &
   round   in   mimicry   of   itself   of   a   linear   thing.

Digital clocks cast no shadows   therefore   like the shades whom Dante
    encounters   in Purgatory   no Matter.   Clocks with hands
Now   that's another story.   Each minute a form.   Each one

   leading another on.   8:38   for example   & 38 seconds!
     A chance minute.   A Previously merging into   Afterwards.
   A juncture in which   one   must   be   willing.   An imperceptible shift
       of light on   any object it strives to illumine.

Any book of hours hides in it   a diary of minutes   a volume   (a reading)   of days.
        A season.   Its feast.
     Among its *am*'s & *pm*'s   Winter hunkers speechless against
       any given minute   its birth   –rushing.   Fallen.

Faced with 8:38

Faced with 8:38 (its form & function,
its deliberate countenance), anything I could say turns
cheap & aphoristic. Blush & stumble words
armored in intent.

My time spent (spine bent) in the brevity of
this 8:38 – in the linger & lull of its quick arms
– has been Auspicious. A piece of luck.
& Opportune.

Because time can instruct. Is.
Is always, in a sense, 8:38 & never
a finished thing. . . . Time is becoming less
rigid or more so.

Any form tends to become its own
function & carries within it (clutched
or cradled) a miniature of its own
destruction.

Movement & form are not the same
thing unless movement is given form
(is formed by & accepts
the gesture).

What have I done?   (for example)

My eyes opened just as the bedroom
clock (digital) configured as if on ice 8:38.
Day, thus far, appears convex & not
altogether unpleasant.

On us too

        On us too
beings & things
cast no shadow

        morning is slim
sunless & nervous
a minute belies me

        a minute betrays
a hand's tiniest
hesitation

        in this kitchen
now
toast toasting in a toaster

        & time's utter

refusal to obey
the promise of its own

         consistency, its own
myth

as if planning
already

         the daily, the small
celebrations
kept secret & to itself

while I have   coffee & toast
8:38 prefers   tea & eggs

Mary Molinary
Beloit Poetry Journal
Volume 56, Number 1
Fall 2005

Very Hot Day

I know what's going to happen
to those two plastic produce bags of crushed ice
I perched atop the garden wall:
one's floppy, droopy, flabby,
its overhanging pooch of ice-melt
already about to pull the whole bag down
into the dirt, bursting it, turning it
into a fistful of filthy gummy polyethelene;
the other's centered, poised – even
its ice-melt seems to know where to settle
so the bag stays upright and stable:
if it were a person, he'd radiate
smiling confidence and good health,
a team player wanting only to be useful,
to stand as an example of how to adjust
conflicting parts of himself for the general good.
His effortless balance and bright red twisty-tie
might seem flashy and arrogant
were he not so persistently mindful
that he shares the other bag's fate.
How could he not, since they're almost touching?
He'd have to be completely oblivious
not to witness the moment his twin
plops into the dirt.
He'd have to know he's heading there, too,
no matter how solid he feels at present –
that even now he's really broken and helpless
and destined for the recycle bin
where like an omniscient god I throw
useless used bags for crushed ice
the butcher gives me to keep my raw meat
safe while I drive home on a very hot day.

Michael Ryan
The American Poetry Review
May/June 2005

To Failure

You and I are like a marriage of convenience
between two down-on-their-luck families,
the Eastmans and the Roebucks, or the Nixons
and the Goldwaters. We don't care for each other,

but I have a bottle of wine and you have a corkscrew.
I have a pack of cigarettes and you have a lighter.
We agree to sheathe our teeth, drink the wine,
smoke, kiss. A day becomes a night, one night

becomes two nights. I get out of bed, put on my boxers,
shorts, and a white T-shirt silk-screened with a photo
of construction workers eating lunch atop a skyscraper
in 1932. The sun is hot when I walk around the corner

to withdraw twenty dollars from a bank machine.
The dots of gum on the cement sidewalk look like
an exercise in a child's book. Connecting the dots
to see where they lead seems luckier than going back.

Tim Skeen
Prairie Schooner
Volume 79, Number 3
Fall 2005

Trying to Be Penitent

on the leather pews,
the wood was coming through,
so I thought only of my knees,
not his heroic finish
hammered to his handiwork,
not of the gory suds
that according to the sermoner
rivered from
his sacred liver

and ran downhill
into the mob that
was there to see God die
and on the under-card
the two common thieves
he hung between,
his arms extended like a politician
or emcee –

just two village punks
like the guys I grew up with,
Crazy Harry
who set houses on fire,
Barbone, who unsnugged
lug nuts and watched the cars
fall off their tires,
or the Jimmy Love that I
hung on the Poe School fence
for swiping my glove.
Glum and unrepentant,
even after he gave in
I kept beating him.

The censors snuffed,
I heard the *Ite, missa est*
and along with the rest
of the thoughtless and quick-heeled
rushed to the doors, sun-framed,

thanking the empty sky
that I would not that day
be with Him in Paradise.

J. T. Barbarese
The Black Beach
University of North Texas Press

Stroke

Johnny Cloud had one the summer
he was camp counselor,
spaghetti he'd just eaten
all over the boards of our cabin
on that perfect day of sun and no wind.
Back from the hospital months
later, he was quiet, carried
his elbow out, hand down, always
making a left, dragging
his foot, every step
a stumble. I see this
when you hold a spoon, pencil.

Everybody in the family died
of one, my grandmother signing
a funeral guest register, my
grandfather lying on his rake
in the back yard for hours,
his white temple stained violet.
The doctor sees a river
of blood, flowing through the mind,
growing up through the brain
like a tree through a house,
and any of the limbs,
to the twig, to the bud,
might blossom to fill a room
we need, be an *episode*,
like one part of a life story,
as if the longest branch were in
your palm, as if on the scan looking
down through every slice of that
tree, from tip to root,
there were rings I couldn't see.

William Greenway
Fishing at the End of the World
Word Press

Racial Profile #2

You bring out the Jamaica in me
The killer hotsauce hot head knock
Dead slap face yell bellow yellow
Curry goat and ackee egomania
Mango maniac attack smack codfish
Salt to shrink a hippopotamus
In me

You bring out the best behavior Sunday
Rice and peas in coconut oil and ganja
Fantasy and Arawak free or gone
To Rasta fury and a cane-field
Flaming slave revolt
In me

Me no repent
Me no relent

You bring out the Jamaica in me
The violent cradle for my temper
Tantrum reggae and banana basic no way
Blues in me

You bring out the typhoon flinging hurricane swinging
Doors and roof tops got to go
In me

Me no repent
Me no relent

You/Calypso
Palm tree dirt path to the big wink
Crocodile the now
You see me now you
Won't believe
How close how hot
How kiss the queen how
Crop the king Jamaica
I can really be

You betta to make room for the mongoose poet
Spill no relent and no repent juice
Over you over
And over you over
And over
And over
you

June Jordan
Directed by Desire: The Collected Poems of June Jordan
Edited by Jan Heller Levi and Sara Miles
Copper Canyon Press

Sursum Corda

a housing development in Northwest Washington, DC

The hart leaps.

Through the bracken of Children's Island, its sedge and mallow,
through the brush and tangle of Stadium Narrows,
the hart leaps.

Past the Canada geese gulls starlings sparrows & crows,
past flea market flannels cottons linens corduroys,
blooms of rust curling over cast-iron stump-legged stoves,
teflon peeling off bundt pans frying pans & bake trays,
the hart leaps.

Across grooved tailgates of pick-ups & second-life trucks
& white scoop-lipped concrete deadweights of a Grand Prix track
that roared once into the records & now sits silent,
skirting winter-bald grass & a golf club's loopy fence,
indefensible, uphill on icebroken pavement
& a bookhouse for bombed-out Beirut, past 19th &
M where a five-inch blade five times five days ago was
driven into a delivery man in busy
daylight, the hart leaps.

Into seven-square square blocks of gridded deerpark moor,
of hunting, coney-poaching, Crown lands & highwaymen,
a wilderness for the staking and taking, neither
National Arboretum nor oaks of Dumbarton
but *Sursum Corda*, that they shall be lifted up, here
in Jubal, glory & comfort, where more are fallen
& dead more quickly than stroke, than shock, in this red square

& plaza of promises, catholic talismen
of fair winds & crossings for a Northwest Passage, for
a land of lows, storm fronts, mortuary cold, a land
of the could-have-been, streets earstruck with seven-on-four
beats of blood in the hot walls of ears, blood like lichen
on stubble of old sidewalk & cyclone fence under
tundra skies of lost dominion, lost direction
from courtyard to courtyard, gravel to cement, through beer-
bottle grass to Coke-green glass to yellow-white to brown
to blue, the hart leaps.

Greatgrandmas look through torn curtains to see him rampant,
tearing through bushes, his horns flashing with raw bonelight,
an emergency of wonder, brown-red, ambulant,
their heraldic stag of tincture sanguine & fur bright
with sweat & flecks of foil. Now the children chase after,
fingers flared from their heads like horns, prancing in his wake,
or fists to their mouths for the loud brass of hunting horns,
dashing in greyhound frenzy & whippet crazy-eights.
What's happening here? Who is running the tapestry
through the looms, the stag around the tight bends & charges
of the NW, over fine dust, spent shells, & dark green
mazes with ancient etched numbers & flowered marges?
What game is afoot? In their black-&-whites the Finest
hear the sightings crackle in over their speakers, call
for soft-poison darts, doctors, game wardens, riot vests,
revving their engines for what may come down after all
to high-speed pursuit, wrong-ways on one-way avenues,
dashes over medians & dividers. Copters

are circling now, networks covering this breaking news
as his hooves strike blue fires across the faulted curbs
of the Project, his horns lit by flashes & first hints
of sunset, his head twisting in a mounting panic,
his sense of true north lost among the bands of children,
the rush of rotors, district captains hustling manic
in their blinds, lips to bullhorns, blue flash red flash white flash,
lost among the pounding bass of boom-car double amps,
out of sight of tall trees, beyond salt lick or high grass,
he stops, breathing harder than first thunder, & stamps. Stamps.
The whippet-children stand stockstill, wary as old hounds.
Dealers drop their seal-tite bags. Traffic slows to a cough.
Copters hover in five o'clock suspense. . . . *Bring him down*,
hears a crouching man through an earpiece small as what's left
of shooting & stars once they fall to earth, & the heart

                                              leaps.

Hillel Schwartz
FIELD
Number 72
Spring 2005

The Chair She Sits In

I've heard this thing where, when someone dies,
People close up all the holes around the house –

The keyholes, the chimney, the windows,
Even the mouths of the animals, the dogs and the pigs.

It's so the soul won't be confused, or tempted.
It's so when the soul comes out of the body it's been in

But that doesn't work anymore,
It won't simply go into another one

And try to make itself at home,
Pretending as if nothing happened.

There's no mystery – it's too much work to move on.
It isn't anybody's fault. A soul is like any of us.

It gets used to things, especially after a long life.
The way I sit in my living-room chair,

The indentation I have put in it now
After so many years – that's how I understand.

It's my chair,
And I know how to sit in it.

Alberto Ríos
The Theater of Night
Copper Canyon Press

Blue Umbrella

Deer Isle

Kai says, "Here, let me fix that, you don't know
how." This elegant mechanism, a present
from my daughter, topped by its own wind hat,
engineered not to turn inside out in nor'easters
or August hurricanes. Ingenious invention of China
and Egypt, emblem of rank in remote antiquity,
collapsible shade, pampering portable sunscreen
at least a millennium before a damp Brit eureka'd
the thought of keeping dry. Bishop's Crusoe
fashioned one on his desolate island, had "such a time"
remembering the way the ribs would go.
Palpable perfection centuries in the making.
Cobalt canopy I left sprung open to dry outdoors,
away from the library's waxed floors. A courtesy,
I thought, and someone's shoved it into a railing,
so one of the little wooden caps that tip the steel ribs
and hold the water-proofed cloth taut, has split.
Now there's a gap in my assurance of shelter.
Ruined, ruined, I think – my small losses

resound in me today as titanic griefs – but Kai –
who makes his art from what you might call nothing –
toothpicks, mussel shells, buttons, discarded books,
garlic stems – who'll find anywhere, in Toronto
or Kowloon or at this island's dump swap shop,
the raw ingredients of his dreamy constructions,
Kai, who knows I'm not "skillful with my hands"
yet hasn't turned from me, Kai, smiling
in his yellow silk quilted jacket, in his black beret
in the rain, holds out the deft hand of friendship
and takes the ultimate umbrella to his work-
bench, carving for me two perfect maple caps,
one for now, one for the future, when he knows
in his heart I'll need another (don't things
always break?) – And won't we two be far apart?

Gail Mazur
Zeppo's First Wife:
New and Selected Poems
The University of Chicago Press

Report from My Own Backyard

October's done its mischief here already.
As has the cat, from the looks of the vole
spinning like a dervish
on the walk near my back door.

A missing foot? A wound? Anything
but ecstasy I can believe. When I box it
for transport to the neighbor's pines, its body
thumps the cardboard. Let's think of this
as a primer. My Own Backyard.
It's where I'm told I should begin.

And it's greedy for attention.
Always the chickadees; sometimes
the finches. I arrange the errant hose
in the tidy coils of my mind.

The lawn chair on its side will gather snow
if it's left to me. I picture myself
going out with the sole purpose
of bringing that chair in. I should begin
in my own backyard

where the plumbing
of the recently departed
boiler flails. There's no shame in devotion
to my little nation of stinks and groans,

this compost pile feeding skunks –
the hegemony of the hedge
on one side, the clear boundary
of my refusal to mow on the other.

I could die here, so convenient a plot.
I could wave my apron like a flag. Come home!
Come home! Leave others
to their yards and bones. There's no horror
in matched dogs walking you evenings

like a philosophy. Bury me by
the quid pro quo of the quince,
the shed's *Don't ask me* shrug.

Paula Closson Buck
AGNI 62

Used One Speed, Princeton

I painted my bike purple,
it's finding a brown to fade to.
Along the long slow curve of streets
gelato-colored houses change in dusk
to colors of dove. On my one speed, life is plain.
Here the mudflats are called a river. I am feeling
new muscles in my thighs. My fat fenders
guard me from mud-splat. Look at these tires:
wide as trenches. My second-grade teacher said
"sit up straight." My ex-fiancé used to
put his hand through his hair,
make a fist, say "that's just them
trying to keep the working class docile."
The houses dim, colors of soap, the shaped kind
you put in little dishes, that shrink and melt
to goo. I sometimes feel rather shaky
but that's OK. I guard against regret,
disapproval, those middle-aged emotions.
I am still young, I feel I am. If I wanted I could
ride no-hands, my bike so steady, arms out
like that guy in Goya's *Third of May, 1808*,
with the white shirt, his eyes wide open,
facing death. I don't.   I squint my eyes
against gnats. And so, and so, I was saying,
when a certain feeling comes over me,
something that feels like foolish bravery,
I glide, concede, I sit straight up.

Daisy Fried
My Brother Is Getting Arrested Again
University of Pittsburgh Press

One-Time Use

Camera in a twelve-room house.
Twenty-four exposures, one-time use.

Cobwebs and a sable wrap,
diaphragm and Dimetapp,

wrenches and yellow quarts,
Clan of the Cave Bear, Torts,

diplomas, "Girls of the Big Ten,"
sunlight and gin,

china and Queen Anne chairs,
carpet and tears,

shotgun and NordicTrack,
white slips and black,

two angels on a shelf.
Your wife. Yourself.

Richard D. Allen
The Hudson Review
Volume LVIII, Number 1
Spring 2005

Feeding the Fire

Down the chute the coal chunks come, black and brittle
from time's press, packed with essence of dim forests,
funk of flora, fungiforms, relics of the Paleozoic
destined for my furnace, fire-bellied Baal that warms
the innards of this house.
                              I toss the flame a shovel load
and feel the blaze of opaque past transfigured into infrared,
then kick shut the furnace door and wipe the smudge
of pitch-black dust that seams the lifeline of my palm.

Edison Jennings
The Kenyon Review
New Series, Volume XXVII Number 4
Fall 2005

Aristophanes at the Woodpile

The wind-fall Maple yields
a dozen stove wood lengths,
pale gray cylinders whose
dull exteriors belie
sweet white wood inside.
Each free rolling piece upended
shows a brown bull'seye.

Zeus wields his axe. Split
by well-aimed blows, the right,
the left halves fall away,
each with its streak of broken
heart wood. Each no longer may
roll free but lies where chance
left it in the crisscross piles.

Each half stacked neatly but alone.
For each the other's lost among
similar, indifferent sticks,
each with its emptiness,
helpless – unless chance matches
their desire and Eros
joins them in a single fire.

Robert Chute
Beloit Poetry Journal
Volume 56, Number 2
Winter 2005/06

Snow

Some days
The snow has taken me in
To know the time of snow, to live
Inside a world so quiet

Its music
Is all a shimmering. Some evenings
When quite alone
I turn off every light

And watch the snow
Enjoy the dark, moving lushly
Through spiky air,
Finding more time

In time
Than when I stretch myself
And am
My father's father. Oh yes,

There is
A sparkling choir, there surely is,
And dark ice air
Through which we fall

Kevin Hart
Harvard Review
Number 29, 2005

Mycorrhizae

When you dig up a tree,
keep some soil around the roots,
webby strands
wrap the taproot, the calm anchor, reach
horizontal through duff and toad dung,
damp mould. Things move so
discreetly sometimes,
I didn't even notice.
A tiger's ear flares in shade,
was that the water molecule's
elemental split? The sleight of hand
described on page twenty? No, not exactly,
you prop a shingle barrier up
to shelter a wind-torn cabbage sprout.
Strawberries edge the bed, an upside down
pot keeps rain from the post hole,
another adage proved: plant
at the new moon,
a stitch in time saves nine,
if you must leave, don't
go bare, take some dirt with you.

Talvikki Ansel
Poetry
Volume CLXXXVI, Number 3
June 2005

Army Tales

The boy who drowned in the bog, the boy caught in the rotors, the boy who laughed too loud –

The boy who swallowed the bee that stung the throat –

The rip cord worked, but the parachute fluttered weakly above him and would not bloom –

He put his foot down in the foreign grass and heard a click, as of metal on metal. When he lifted that foot –

Sometimes it is a cold day and the clouds rain toxin over the boys on the base –

Sometimes, they don't know they're being watched, leaning against their packs, asleep like that –

One more, one more, he said. *One more all around* – And the assembled clapped for him, they clapped, he put his money down and smiled because they loved him –

Sometimes a boy thinks he is unloved, so he retires to a dark tent where he will not be disturbed –

Then, the cells wink out like lights on a tall office building in a strange city at dusk –

His friends said it was a sad day, it was very sad. They thought he'd been kidding, they told him not to laugh like that –

You pull the string and out it blooms –

And what was he doing off the base late at night? What was he doing on the open water, in the plane, driving so fast down unfamiliar roads? His mother –

Someone would tell her. Someone would write her a letter, thank god. There's a template for that –

A guy who puts your name on the hard drive, a distant office, a simple program and printer –

You punch in the name and out it comes.

Kevin Prufer
Colorado Review
Volume XXXII, Number 2
Summer 2005

New Year, with Nipperkin

And so the world begins again
In mild disarray
Where the best laid plans of mice and men
It's said, "gang aft agley."

"Gang aft agley" – that sounds just right –
Strangulated, glottal,
Where violence meets backwardness
Summarily throttled.

So merrily and merrily
The Monday doth embark
Us on another work whose week
Will leave us in the dark,

A drink in hand and Parkinson's
Or worse, maybe, to stir
The ice into its carillon
Of Larkinsense and myrrh:

More light! More weight! More love! Less hate!
The Mass, the Seder, ah
The tools we use to disconfuse
Ourselves, etc.

And so, to bed. I draw the shade.
Should auld acquaintance croak
He's none of mine, nor Auld Lang Syne,
Whoever *he* is.   :) *

* joke

Richard Kenney
Antioch Review
Volume 64, Number 1
Winter 2006

Sylvia

Across a space peopled with stars I am
laughing while my sides ache for existence
it turns out is profound though the profound
because of time it turns out is an illusion
and all of this is infinitely improbable
given the space, for which I gratefully lie
in three feet of snow making a shallow grave
I would have called an angel otherwise and
think of my own rapturous escape from
living only as dust and dirt, little sister.

Gerald Stern
Everything Is Burning
W. W. Norton & Company

NOTE:
Sylvia refers to Sylvia Stern, my older sister, dead in 1933, at age nine.

Charles Street, Late November

A friend on the edge of death tap-taps
his way, cane-first, to the apothecary.
My arm is the apple branch at his side,
his hand more oriole than invalid.
Ever elegant, he wears a wide-brimmed hat
and mackintosh, pausing often to deplore
the self-indulgence of this wealthy corridor:
the French provincial rosewood perfume box
lined in velvet, "a little coffin for scents,"
and the Portuguese linen smocks
embroidered with ducklings
"who'll get their feet wet more often
than the poor heiresses for whom
these dresses will be bought."
At the corner, a pair of border collies
who seem to have just steered a herd
of sheep back up Mt. Vernon Street
bound to a halt at my friend's feet.
They admire each other, this man
and the neighborhood's working dogs
caught in the thrill of a fresh task.
Their names fall softly from his lips
as he struggles to remove one glove
so they may lick his fingers.
We continue over crazed brick.
Inside the narrow shop that smells of chocolate
and cellophane-wrapped cordwood,
he glides by the pharmacist and dwells
in the stationery aisle; I wait as he chooses
a pocket date book for the coming year.

Erica Funkhouser
Sou'wester
Fall 2005

Keepsake

We had our days, didn't we – sun-stained,
hand-rubbed, pieced and plighted in some massing tale
I'd just begun to see the pattern of.
But we were the birds, too, starving in the woods,
ravening up the crumbs we dropped behind
till we were utterly lost (there was that failed
love, a music box you couldn't fix and I
couldn't, our griefs jangling us, dividing).
Where did you go, wood nymph, your huge, hurt eyes
that saw too much, fluttering in the weeds? –
You always moved moth-wise, in sudden juttings, gusts,
exaltations, long self-banishing silence.
Come back to me sometimes. I wander now too,
am a shadow with you here in this other life.

l.s.w. 1965-2001

Philip White
Quarterly West #60
Summer 2005

Wishful Rhetoric

Finis. I love the oh-so-postmodern opening –
the reversal of expectations intimating a fresh start,
as does potty-training or the pre-dinner after-dinner mint.
After all, in this way the end's a beginning.

So *Finis.* There now, the daisies' clean faces
need never wrinkle, their eyes never shut,
and the plump clump swaying in May breeze
need never dismantle June's skeletal erector set.

That's that. So the orchard's Jonathan need not
drop and rot, the iris's plush petals might
always enshrine its flushed lips, and the lilac
(my favorite) can spend its profligate scent

without fear of overdraft. Breathe in and forget
the out. I am the bank, the root, the fat honeycomb.
I am the aphid milking an everlasting tit.
There now, I'll make the twenty calls from home,

each beginning, "My father died last night."

Kevin Stein
American Ghost Roses
The University of Illinois Press

"Off in the darkness hourses moved restlessly"

– a typo in Clifford Simak's *A Heritage of Stars*

We believed they were horses; and so
we saddled up, we rode expectantly
through the long day and into the night.
Then we dismounted; and slept; and still
they continued to carry us
–the hours. They wouldn't stop.
They carried us clean away.

Albert Goldbarth
Beloit Poetry Journal
Volume 56, Number 1
Fall 2005

The Unlasting

I

Like a vain man practicing a vain art
Born out of failure – not the grand failure
Of the Will or the Imagination,

But on a more human scale: *what happened?*
What happened to the incidental life
You try to make up, though it falls apart?

Each year I come again to where I am.
What happened to that place I meant to make,
That whole of which I meant to be a part,

A whole with space for other people too?
I don't know. The solace of a daily
Hall of mirrors and the nightly bedlam

Of my own dreams – they gradually dissolve
Into a pleasant day in early spring,
A watercolor sky and leafless trees,

All waiting. What I want is what it gives,
Which ought to be enough for me for now –
My strategy is simply to resolve

To see it through, whatever it might bring,
And hope that something *other* should emerge,
That words that come to me along the way

Make up a document that chronicles
A solitary life, bounded by hope.
And so I offer you these rites of spring.

II

A certain life begins and ends with God,
Not as a tangible reality,
But in the abstract, as a nagging sense

Of something lacking, or of something else
Remaining to be said beyond the facts.
The world is all that is the case, complete

In itself, with nothing else beyond it.
Slowly, as it attempts to take it in,
The soul, confronting something so immense,

Is reduced to an insignificance
From which it rises once again in thought
Until at last its triumph is concrete

– That's the delusion: of another way
Of living both within and through the world
That makes experience a sacrament

And intimates a vision of a life
Too vast for its surroundings, magnified
By the endless struggle to make it fit.

Wittgenstein again: "Running against the
Walls of our cage is perfectly hopeless."
But it stands as a living "document

Of a tendency in the human mind
Which I cannot help respecting deeply.
I would not for my life ridicule it."

Could *that* have been my life? It isn't now.
The truth is that I'm lackadaisical,
Content to let the moments come and go

Without a thought for what the years might bring
Or what comes afterwards. Like everyone,
I suppose, I daydream about music

And sex and food; my faults are common ones;
My virtues too. As for mortality
And eternity, all I really know

Is what I've read, which isn't very much.
Poetry helps, but usually conveys
The bare sense of life at its most basic.

I feel like someone waiting to begin
A story without a real ending,
Opening in the middle of the way

And going on from there, page by page
Throughout the night, until the sun comes up
And it's time to start all over again.

Beneath it all I feel the silent rage
Of the unspoken, what gets left unsaid
In the narrative of the everyday:

That here and now can be a prison too,
That of the man who tries to hide himself
Behind the transparent walls of his cage.

IV

I think that it's impossible to give
An explanation of experience
That captures how it feels and what it is

Sub specie aeternitatis, something
Seen from deep space, from just above the earth,
Or even from this city where I live

And where I find myself adrift and free,
Making my way along a busy street
In April, moving with the speed of song

Across a page, with visions of people
Coming as close to me as my own name,
But remaining oblivious of me.

Is there a measure of experience?
Some change that it effects, an altered sense
Of life that follows in its aftermath?

Or is there something it aspires to,
Some changeless ideal it contemplates,
To which it promises obedience?

I think it vanishes before our eyes,
Like something that had never even been.
The day begins in waiting, in the hope

That what I felt once I might feel again
– A fallacy completely obvious,
Yet one so difficult to realize.

V

And so I find myself inhabiting
A kind of no-man's-land between the thoughts
Of earth and heaven, living on the line

Between a once and future life, between
The passive and the possible, through words
That see through both of them and see them through.

I know they're both absurd. The question
Isn't of what to think or what to do,
But what to do without. The choice is mine,

I'd like to think, and whether to abjure
Those fantasies is simply up to me.
It's not that easy though. For if I knew

What lay beyond them or could take their place
In the mythologies I listen to
To tell me what to feel and how to see,

This fear of letting go might dissipate
Like this morning's fog, leaving me at peace
And reconciled to what I had become.

A picture held us captive: but my dream
Is to walk away from it, emerging
Into a space with room enough for me

And me alone. I want to lose myself
In what I've thought and felt and seen, and then
Avert my eyes and let that kingdom come.

VI

And then to my astonishment it did.
Time passed. I found myself remembering
A day in college, then another day,

All real days made up of accidents
And things and people that I'd really known,
And places where I literally had lived

And which had been as much a part of me
As this apartment now. For by assembling
All of them into a rambling story

Ranging over distant times and places,
I'd given them a being of their own,
A life that felt continuous with mine.

And suddenly the light that filled the trees
Came from a summer forty years ago.
An ordinary April day assumed

The effusive California colors
Of an autumn afternoon, when the sun
Has burned away the early morning haze.

Could that be what Proust meant? I think it is:
That time, which seems relentless in its slow
Approach to anonymity and death,

Is impotent against the will of art;
That nothing disappears; that once begun
Its epiphany goes on forever.

He asks you to believe that a release
From the constraints of time, a quiet state
In which the present and the past seem merged,

Opens on a suffocating bedroom
Furnished with the past, with sempiternal
Moments laid up in a sanctuary

Outside of time, or better still, submerged
Beneath the currents of the everyday –
A transport ending in deliverance,

Like a journey down an estuary
Flowing at last into the open sea.
I don't believe it. Yesterday is fixed,

And yet its possibilities remain,
Its sense of feeling "absolutely safe,
Whatever happens," whether on the way

To the store, or sitting on a park bench
Looking at the cars, the clouds, that airplane
In a slow descent towards Mitchell Field.

And even in the middle of the day
This sense is of the presence of the past,
But in an immanent, more human form –

Not as a hidden heart that lies concealed
Beneath the skin of ordinary life,
But here in its moments, which come and go

And where this daydreaming finally ends –
Not in a quiet recess in the mind,
But on an afternoon that seems a vast

Cathedral brimming with an earthly light
That shows things as they are, and lets them go.
Why do we want to bring them back again?

What does it *mean,* "the presence of the past,"
If not a pang at how things disappear,
A love of the unlasting, brought to earth

By the pervasiveness of change? And when,
In a fleeting moment of distraction,
The light seems that of a distant morning

In New York, an afternoon in high school
In the shade of a bungalow, it's not
That they'd been waiting but that they were gone.

These things were good because they had to die.
They vanish, and the traces that they leave
Are part of nature too, a part of us

That wants to keep them as we wish they were.
I took the past for granted. I forgot
How much of it we fabricate, how much

Of my life is actually a story
Mixing what I want and what I believe
With some words that retell it from within.

IX

The first failure, from which the others flow,
Is to live entirely in a world
Of your own making, and to live alone.

Whatever else I started out to find,
What I've arrived at is a kind of place
– A temporary one – I never left,

That I can neither alter nor postpone.
But it's not going to last: like everything
Under the sun a poem has its day

Or year or years, and then – what? Time is theft,
But in the long run what it takes away
Comes back as something numinous and strange,

That simply having lived through seems enough.
I know the tone, and what it tries to say.
I know the measure of reality

Isn't what I say to myself, but what
Another person tries to say to me,
Who turns to me and smiles, and turns away.

There is an air of unreality
About this place, as though I looked at it
Through someone else's eyes. And what I see

Is nothing but an ordinary day
Transformed, unlike all those I've known before,
And so strange. And I think it's wonderful.

X

Let it get dark, and the inessential
Noises fade into the mild April night,
Leaving just the houses, a hill, some trees,

And stretching out as far as you can see
A lake illuminated by the moon,
By the moon illusion. Low in the sky,

As though hanging just above the water,
It shines at the end of a path of light
Beginning at the shore and flowing east.

Ascending, it gets smaller, finally
Becoming, like a spell that breaks too soon,
A stone in the impersonal night sky.

When I was a boy my bedroom window
Looked out upon a range of soft brown hills.
Beyond them lay the desert and the East,

A country cloaked in a green I'd never
Seen until I took the bus to college
That brought me in the end to where I am –

An odd place, yet one I must have chosen
Long ago, like a promise time fulfills
In passing, that comes too late, that leaves me

Floating in the air between a fleeting
Glimpse of nothing and the common knowledge
That lay waiting for me beyond the hills.

John Koethe
The Kenyon Review
New Series, Volume XXVIII Number 1
Winter 2006

Darkness Starts

A shadow in the shape of a house
slides out of a house
and loses its shape on the lawn.

Trees seek each other
as the wind within them dies.

Darkness starts inside of things
but keeps on going when the things are gone.

Barefoot careless in the farthest parts of the yard
children become their cries.

Christian Wiman
Hard Night
Copper Canyon Press

Tree Ghost

There's a rush, a rustle
among branches of a conifer,
& then mutable silence rushes in
like after a fight or making love.
The wings settle. The third eye
blindfolded. Hunger always speaks
the same language. Branches shudder
overhead, & the snowy owl's wingspan
seems to cool off the August night
with a breathing in & breathing out.

I close my eyes & can still see
the three untouched mice dead
along the afternoon footpath.
The screeching nest is ravenous.
The mother's claws grab a limb.
Now, what I know makes me look down
at the ground. I can almost feel
how the owl's beauty scared the mice
to death, how the shadow of her wings
was a god passing over the grass.

Yusef Komunyakaa
TriQuarterly 121

Death, Etc.

I have lived my whole life with death, said William Maxwell,
aetat 91, and haven't we all. Amen to that.
It's all right to gutter out like a candle but the odds are better

for succumbing to a stroke or pancreatic cancer.
I'm not being gloomy, this bright September
when everything around me shines with being:

hummingbirds still raptured in the jewelweed,
puffballs humping up out of the forest duff
and the whole voluptuous garden still putting forth

bright yellow pole beans, deep-pleated purple cauliflowers,
to say nothing of regal white corn that feeds us
night after gluttonous night, with a slobber of butter.

Nevertheless, what Maxwell said speaks to my body's core,
this old body I trouble to keep up the way
I keep up my two old horses, wiping insect deterrent

on their ears, cleaning the corners of their eyes,
spraying their legs to defeat the gnats, currying burrs
out of their thickening coats. They go on grazing thoughtlessly

while winter is gathering in the wings. But it is not given
to us to travel blindly, all the pasture bars down,
to seek out the juiciest grasses, nor to predict

which of these two will predecease the other or to anticipate
the desperate whinnies for the missing that will ensue.
Which of us will go down first is also not given,

a subject that hangs unspoken between us
as with Oedipus, who begs Jocasta not to inquire further.
Meanwhile, it is pleasant to share opinions and mealtimes,

to swim together daily, I with my long slow back and forths,
he with his hundred freestyle strokes that wind him alarmingly.
A sinker, he would drown if he did not flail like this.

We have put behind us the State Department tour
of Egypt, Israel, Thailand, Japan that ended badly
as we leapt down the yellow chutes to safety after a botched takeoff.

We have been made at home in Belgium, Holland, and Switzerland,
narrow, xenophobic Switzerland of clean bathrooms and much butter.
We have travelled by Tube and Metro *o'er the realms of gold*

paid obeisance to the Wingèd Victory and the dreaded Tower,
but now it is time to settle as the earth itself settles
in season, exhaling, dozing a little before the fall rains come.

Every August when the family gathers, we pose
under the ancient willow for a series of snapshots,
the same willow, its lumpish trunk sheathed in winking aluminum

that so perplexed us forty years ago, before we understood
the voracity of porcupines. Now hollowed by age and marauders,
its aluminum girdle painted dull brown, it is still leafing

out at the top, still housing a tumult of goldfinches. We try to hold still
and smile, squinting into the brilliance, the middleaged children,
the grown grandsons, the dogs of each era, always a pair

of grinning shelter dogs whose long lives are but as grasshoppers
compared to our own. We try to live gracefully
and at peace with our imagined deaths but in truth we go forward

stumbling, afraid of the dark,
of the cold, and of the great overwhelming
loneliness of being last.

Maxine Kumin
Alaska Quarterly Review
Volume 22, Numbers 1 & 2
Spring & Summer 2005

Appalachian Farewell

Sunset in Appalachia, bituminous bulwark
Against the western skydrop.
An Advent of gold and green, an Easter of ashes.

If night is our last address,
This is the place we moved from,
Backs on fire, our futures hard-edged and sure to arrive.

These are the towns our lives abandoned,
Wind in our faces,
The idea of incident like a box beside us on the Trailways' seat.

And where were we headed for?
The country of Narrative, that dark territory
Which spells out our stories in sentences, which gives them an end and beginning . . .

Goddess of Bad Roads and Inclement Weather, take down
Our names, remember us in the drip
And thaw of wintery mix, remember us when the light cools.

Help us never to get above our raising, help us
To hold hard to what was there,
Orebank and Reedy Creek, Surgoinsville down the line.

Charles Wright
The Wrong End of the Rainbow
Quarternote Chapbook Series #4
Sarabande Books

Prescience

We speak of Heaven who have not yet accomplished
even this, the holiness of things
precisely as they are, and never will!

Before death was I saw the shining wind.
To disappear, today's as good a time as any.
To surrender at last

to the vast current –
And look, even now there's still time.
Time for the glacial, cloud-paced

soundless music to unfold once more.
Time, inexhaustible wound, for
your unwitnessed and destitute coronation.

Franz Wright
God's Silence
Alfred A. Knopf, Publisher

Big Doors

I have seen with my own eyes doors so massive
that two men would have been required
to push open just one of them.
Bronze, grating over stone sills, or made of wood
from trees now nearly extinct.

Many things never to be seen again!
The fury of cavalry attacking at full gallop.
Little clouds of steam rising
from horse droppings
on most of the world's streets once.

Rooms amber with lamplight
perched above those streets.
Pilgrimage routes smoky with torchlight
from barony to principality through forests
that stood as a dark uncut authority.

A story that begins "Once upon a time."
Messengers, brigands, heralds
in a world unmapped from village to village.
Legends and dark misinformation,
graveyards crowded with ghosts.

And when the rider from that story at last arrives,
gates open at midnight to receive him.
Two men, two men we will never know,
lean into the effort of
pushing open each big door.

Richard Tillinghast
AGNI 62

To You

Beginning on a line by Silvio Rodríguez

How will it taste – the beer the gravedigger
will drink after bestowing your dirt coat?
What will he say – you keeled the outrigger
too south, & when the breakers rolled, no boats
heard your Mayday? & will he ask his friends
at the bar – if someone calls a Mayday
& there is no one at the other end
of any radio, did Kevin A.
González really exist? O second
person, what would you do without you? Where
would Kevin A. González hide? Our bond
is over. The red of the rockets' glare
has faded. Your grave has been dug. Gone too
are the days when I tried to speak through you.

Kevin A. González
Poetry
Volume CLXXXVII, Number 2
November 2005

To the Soul

Is anyone there
if so
are you real
either way are you
one or several
if the latter
are you all at once
or do you
take turns not answering

is your answer
the question itself
surviving the asking
without end
whose question is it
how does it begin
where does it come from
how did it ever
find out about you
over the sound
of itself
with nothing but its own
ignorance to go by

W. S. Merwin
Migration: New and Selected Poems
Copper Canyon Press

White Heron Pond

Either the cicadas hushed,
or I fell asleep
as they kept on.
>   But I go on
>   hearing them

in willows, in wild ancient oaks,
in the slow orbit
of my sleep or waking,
>   where I lie beside
>   White Heron Pond.

Wind whirls through the marsh grasses.
And the slender,
glass wings
>   of ten thousand
>   insects flare

in the shadows and circulating air,
the throb and ebb
of their song.
>   *Who says poetry must*
>   *stick to the theme?*

asks Su Shih when he looks again
at the painting
he loves –
>   branches of
>   flowering plum.

Burrowing out of
soft ground,
up to the highest limbs,
>   the cicadas
>   mate and sing,

then bear their young, who fall
to earth
to nest, asleep,
>   for seventeen
>   years.

Over algae and moss
of the pond's
still surface,
>   over fields of beans
>   and sweet fescue,

this song wavers and floats –
so Su Shih, after years
migrating
>   the provinces, a minor
>   official, turns

into Su Tung-p'o, the poet –
or as now, like
the swirl of stars,
>   as in my dream
>   or waking,

over sun-tipped blooms, over new pipes
poking through
rye grasses,
>   over paved
>   curbs

running wild into the woods,
the sure, slow
orbit of things
>   becoming
>   the next thing.

David Baker
Midwest Eclogue
W. W. Norton & Company

The Insistence of Beauty

The day before those silver planes
came out of the perfect blue, I was struck
by the beauty of pollution rising
from smokestacks near Newark,
gray and white ribbons of it
on their way to evanescence.

And at impact, no doubt, certain beholders
and believers from another part of the world
must have seen what appeared gorgeous –
the flames of something theirs being born.

I watched for hours – mesmerized –
that willful collision replayed,
the better man in me not yielding,
then yielding to revenge's sweet surge.

The next day there was a photograph
of dust and smoke ghosting a street,
and another of a man you couldn't be sure
was fear-frozen or dead or made of stone,

and for a while I was pleased
to admire the intensity – or was it the coldness? –
of each photographer's good eye.
For years I'd taken pride in resisting

the obvious – sunsets, snowy peaks,
a starlet's face – yet had come to realize
even those, seen just right, can have
their edgy place. And the sentimental,

beauty's sloppy cousin, that enemy,
can't it have a place too?
Doesn't a tear deserve a close-up?
When word came of a fireman

who hid in the rubble
so his dispirited search dog
could have someone to find, I repeated it
to everyone I knew. I did this for myself,
not for community or beauty's sake,
yet soon it had a rhythm and a frame.

Stephen Dunn
The American Poetry Review
July/August 2005

Ars Poetica?

I have always aspired to a more spacious form
that would be free from the claims of poetry or prose
and would let us understand each other without exposing
the author or reader to sublime agonies.

In the very essence of poetry there is something indecent:
a thing is brought forth which we didn't know we had in us,
so we blink our eyes, as if a tiger had sprung out
and stood in the light, lashing his tail.

That's why poetry is rightly said to be dictated by a daimonion,
though it's an exaggeration to maintain that he must be an angel.
It's hard to guess where that pride of poets comes from,
when so often they're put to shame by the disclosure of their frailty.

What reasonable man would like to be a city of demons,
who behave as if they were at home, speak in many tongues,
and who, not satisfied with stealing his lips or hand,
work at changing his destiny for their convenience?

It's true that what is morbid is highly valued today,
and so you may think that I am only joking
or that I've devised just one more means
of praising Art with the help of irony.

There was a time when only wise books were read,
helping us to bear our pain and misery.
This, after all, is not quite the same
as leafing through a thousand works fresh from psychiatric clinics.

And yet the world is different from what it seems to be
and we are other than how we see ourselves in our ravings.
People therefore preserve silent integrity,
thus earning the respect of their relatives and neighbors.

The purpose of poetry is to remind us
how difficult it is to remain just one person,
for our house is open, there are no keys in the doors,
and invisible guests come in and out at will.

What I'm saying here is not, I agree, poetry,
as poems should be written rarely and reluctantly,
under unbearable duress and only with the hope
that good spirits, not evil ones, choose us for their instrument.

Berkeley, 1968

Czełsaw Miłosz
Selected Poems: 1931-2004
Selected by Robert Hass
Ecco
An Imprint of HarperCollins*Publishers*

NOTE:

Translation by Czesław Miłosz and Lillian Vallee.

Testament

. . . that part that
goes nowhere, fits nothing, that
doesn't, wouldn't, isn't, instigates none-
the-

less the speculation of all parts that
are. call it, if

one will, a part so
im-
partial, an anomaly so absolute, that
nothing, if not the breath it-
self, might attain

such resolute autonomy. nothing, that is, if
not the

germinal circulation of
letters
a-
lighting, at last, on
something altogether lighter than the

slightest
increments of
substance itself. there, that
is, where the

rose, so
accorded, might bud ebullient in the very
midst of such
an

inherent socket of
exemption.

Gustaf Sobin
Boston Review
April/May 2005

My Mother's Poem

> Red-winged blackbird, sitting on a stalk,
> What would you say if you could talk?

She showed it to me shyly
After I'd been away for a long time.
She said this was the only one
She'd ever tried to write, and of course
It was only the beginning.

She'd written it on stationery
I'd given her: pastel flowers
In one corner. Far away,
I'd been opening and unfolding
Pages like this for years.

She said she couldn't quite decide
What to say next. She wasn't sure
How it should go on or maybe
It shouldn't, and she was showing me
Because I was supposed to know about poems.

We stood there side by side
At the kitchen sink, looking out the window
At the swamp for a moment, both of us
Wondering how to be inspired
In spite of feeling maybe it didn't matter

To anyone except ourselves
Who could both see those birds hanging on
Sideways to cattail stalks and singing
The one song they seemed to be sure of,
Already knowing the end and how to answer.

David Wagoner
The Hudson Review
Volume LVIII, Number 4
Winter 2006

The Pity of Punctuation

Hoard of words released like manic
spring with its quick gush blooms of bright
where endings have not even a small chance
life forever resurrecting itself without the monster
splotch which when shrunken to depressed
the psychoanalyst calls the period
of realization and the patient hangs on
for her dear however listless
existence like a hyphen at the end
of its rope searching for its dropped
letters like I wait and hold my breath
for my letter that the male carrier might bring
with the possible swerve of love
before any wall of stiff brackets
and the unforgiving is embedded
into the type you know the type

where false hope lies in the dash and never forget

the pun how could one for therein
lived the fun when it was lost inside
me as my body and all punctuation
was temporarily erased eight years ago
same as the symbol of eternity
in April that whore month
with its hoard of all that is
possible while the sun slowly pitched itself
into the lake and he left and suddenly

too many commas crawled in carrying
colons with their screaming litanies of lists
and question marks with *WHYWHYWHY*
on their small hooked spineless backs
and the parade would not stop

until finally the period did roll in so bleak
and yet what a tiny thing it *was*
as I began to feel the fade into
the seamless midnight sky
with my being given
no choice but to curve onto that dot
and disappear with it

Susan Hahn
Self/Pity
Northwestern University Press

The Locust Song

. . . the wise and wry observation which the young William Butler Yeats offered one evening in The Cheshire Cheese to his fellow young poets in the Rhymers Club: "None of us can say who will succeed, or even who has or has not talent. The only thing certain about us is that we are too many."
– Paul Carroll

The tyranny of poets: "Like." O we were like
the infinite regression of roe, in the sex crease
of a sturgeon. We were like – what? like, as numerous
as the stars, the grains of sand, the uses of "like" itself.
Too many of us. Too flakes of snow, too fish
in the deep, too waterbugs of Florida. In the thick air

of the evening Cheese, a muss-haired Willie Yeats stares out
across a bobbing sea of schnockered literary faces
and he sees, as if implied in these, the overmany faces
of the shantytowns, and the Chinese steppes,
and the grim Malthusian banks of the Ganges river
on a holy day . . . too many of us. Those birds

slouched on the wire have served as a bar of music now
in how many poems? as a squadhouse lineup
in how many poems? as heavy portents over
the words in the wire itself, how many times?
Too many many-of-us. That zero now, the "black hole"
of the astronomers . . . by now it's the rose

and the willow and the rainbow and the nightingale
of two generations of us; string theory is easily the sunrise
over the Mediterranean Sea of us. "I think of . . ." then
a historical reference, Mendel, Bruegel, Mata Hari,
how many times? The prize and the prize and the prize.
A swarm of prizes. I think of William Butler Yeats,

a sloshy evening spent in fellowship with his kind. Some
have a scribbled paper with them. Some, a published pamphlet.
All of them have dreams to share. "Inside of every fat man

there's a skinny man waiting to be let out." And inside every
too many of us is a me. Right now, a hundred me
are lifting up their pints and toasting Yeats's observation.

Albert Goldbarth
Poetry
The Humor Issue
Volume CLXXXVI, Number 4
July/August 2005

In a Field

monosyllables

Like stones
in a field.
Small. Large.

There to be used.
To make walls.
To be thrown.

To be held
in our hands.
Light as air.

Or a big thing
that weighs
us down.

I can hide on
the dark side
of this one.

Or tell all.
When I do,
it is not a game.

I pick one up.
Which one is it?
you ask.

I will not tell.
Come here, I say,
and you will see.

You pick one up.
Then I do. Then you.
Then me. Soon

the field is clear.
We have used
each one.

Now
there is
only silence.

Elizabeth Spires
Southwest Review
Volume 90, Number 2 / 2005

Rattlesnakes Hammered on the Wall

Seven of them pinned in blood by
long, shiny tails, three of them still

alive and writhing against the wood,
their heaviness whipping the wall

as they try to break free,
rattles beating in unison,

hisses slowly dying in silence,
the other four hanging stiff

like ropes to another life,
patterns of torn skin dripping

with power and loss, the wonder
of who might have done this

turning to shock as all seven
suddenly come alive when

I get closer, pink mouths
trembling with white fangs,

lunging at me then falling back,
entangled in one another to form

twisted letters that spell a bloody
word I can't understand.

Ray Gonzalez
Consideration of the Guitar:
New and Selected Poems
BOA Editions, Ltd.

Logo Rhythms

+

Judas's cockeyed
kiss or sniper's four quartets –
hoarder's crucifix.

Check out the spoiler
on young Road Runner. Rootster?
Or rototiller.

∞

Complete with caption,
here is the cartoon for which
time wears its goggles.

∝

Open form; closed form –
which is which, these Siamese
twins whose names get switched.

Σ

Some sure-fangled clamp:
certainty snake bit – though not
swallowed – jaws still hinged.

–

Ingot of lead or
of ink, entropy's ally,
plenty's enemy.

~

Ought one not doubt doubt,
a likeness caught here as if
an eyebrow, mirrored?

≅

What is turbulence
to one third is the bottom
of the flag unfurled.

=

Teeth tracks like ski tracks
in the white icing and/or
Oreo itself.

≠

Nothing is nothing
except when it's not something
that crosses the mind.

≡

Ichimi shizen.
Poetry and zen are one.
Shizen ichimi.

x

The times you've sensed how
the straw through the lid might be
like sex with an ex.

∥

O pair of l's, you
who, covert captain, are true
to the rank and file.

⊥

Whenever heaven
plays croquet they borrow from
Euclid his mallet.

π

Bad ass attitude
in coat and hat. Stonehenge pimp
stroll in the abstract.

Δ

So then the voice found
Adam, said, You want I should
draw you a *picture*?

÷

Whose lagoon, what sky
is this reflection of the moon
and solar eclipse?

#

Your call: Italian
ticktacktoe or weighty case
of too much *vino*?

&

Am per *sand?* Even
the eldest of the monks must
have rice in his bowl.

%

Lest you look down on
the blind, know impunity
is a scent its own.

$

His serpent's tally,
Satan's monogram: Snake, one.
Adam? Love. Zilch. None.

Karl Elder
The Minimalist's How-to Handbook
Parallel Press

Lullaby

My little lack-of-light, my swaddled soul,
December baby. Hush, for it is dark,
and will grow darker still. We must embark
directly. Bring an orange as the toll
for Charon: he will be our gondolier.
Upon the shore, the season pans for light,
and solstice fish, their eyes gone milky white,
come bearing riches for the dying year:
solstitial kingdom. It is yours, the mime
of branches and the drift of snow. With shaking
hands, Persephone, the winter's wife,
will tender you a gift. Born in a time
of darkness, you will learn the trick of making.
You shall make your consolation all your life.

Amanda Jernigan
Poetry
Volume CLXXXVII, Number 3
December 2005

Old Age

When it began he was already losing
Interest in the new work by the young.
His own, like X-rays probing, undismayed,
The self whose image brands each dread decade
In lines to which the culture's climbers clung,
Had of a sudden ceased, without his choosing,
To be novel.
                    Less and less inclined
Down darkness at the ends of roads to thrust
His curious, illuminating mind,
For Reality he'd take what he could trust:
The impulse of an art he couldn't stop
Reached back toward all he once by will outgrew
– Nothing so fine now, since his growing up,
No truth as telling as his youth was true.

Daniel Hoffman
Makes You Stop and Think: Sonnets
George Braziller Publishers

Postmortem

Having stood at the edge of a hole dug
As depositary for the body,
I.e., the mortal bit, blip on the screen,
Form given to us, form taken;

                                    having stood
Thus, and watched it lowered, the big box
Waxed and shined to a faux-bronze finish,

I've found words to be shyer than they seem.
Pushed to the edge, they won't leap. In the shade
Of the valley of death, they're toy lamps; they pierce
The wily darkness not. Still,

Bless the nouns and verbs of prayer, the hymnal's
Stodgy rhymes, vanishing in the careless sky
That roofs the bereaved –

                            any sound to efface
The syllable of wind jabbering in the ear,
And on fake metal, the thud of living rose.

Clare Rossini
Lingo
The University of Akron Press

Still Life with Jonquils

The usual bowl of fruit, yes,
and at attention in a blue porcelain vase
wands of jonquils not yet bloomed,

gray-green buds
like translucent cocoons,
their wet and yellow wings

stirring against the thinning threads
of gray, about to give way –
the way a woman whose wrist

has been lightly touched beneath
the starched tablecloth recognizes
a man's invitation, its promise,

as the chatter of dinner guests blurs
into nonsense and she begins to feel
the invisible tug on the knot

fixed at the body's center
waiting
to be undone . . .

The painter knows
what not to execute, knows we bring
our own heat to the canvas,

knowing exactly how
these jonquils would look
if open.

But not letting them.

Andrea Hollander Budy
Arts & Letters
Journal of Contemporary Culture
Issue 13, Spring 2005

Miscegenation

In 1965 my parents broke two laws of Mississippi;
they went to Ohio to marry, returned to Mississippi.

They crossed the river into Cincinnati, a city whose name
begins with a sound like *sin*, the sound of wrong – *mis* in Mississippi.

A year later they moved to Canada, followed a route the same
as slaves, the train slicing the white glaze of winter, leaving Mississippi.

Faulkner's Joe Christmas was born in winter, like Jesus, given his name
for the day he was left at the orphanage, his race unknown in Mississippi.

My father was reading *War and Peace* when he gave me my name.
I was born near Easter, 1966, in Mississippi.

When I turned 33 my father said, *It's your Jesus year – you're the same
age he was when he died.* It was spring, the hills green in Mississippi.

I know more than Joe Christmas did. Natasha is a Russian name –
though I'm not; it means *Christmas child*, even in Mississippi.

Natasha Trethewey
Native Guard
Houghton Mifflin Company

Up Late, Reading Whitman

whose soul was like a spider, but was also like the grass,
and the meteor, and the beach at night, and I
would be honored if my soul was like the neighbor's dog
who tunneled beneath his fence today, black-eyed,
wagging, unclipped toenails clicking on the sidewalk,
all thick tail and barrel chest and neck fat, searching
the hedges for the scent of foe, the site of relief,
for a long-lost loping collie he might have known once
when the day was all sun, and the eternal tennis ball
barely touched the high grass, and the squirrels
couldn't help but admire his splendor,
for happily did he slobber on the sneaker and the hand!

*

My sister who is a young girl again
brings Walt Whitman to the party in the back of the house.

She is so proud. She has kidnapped
the poet and brought him to me – he keeps snapping his fingers,

he still believes he's at the docks.
He walks to the mantle and picks up a trumpet and turns to me.

"You know the song of the soul?" he asks.
"Right," I say, and we step out to the porch where my parents

are sitting in lawn chairs,
and I play perfectly the first four notes of "La Vie en Rose,"

but no one is dancing. "Here give it to me,"
he says. "I fear you are hitting the notes of dream – your eyes

have been the same as closed
most of the time," and his cheeks puff out like old Satchmo's

and I'm happy as a bald-headed man
in a rainstorm of fedoras until the song is over and my parents

sit down and my sister runs up
and tugs on his beard. "But Walt," she says. "Your ride is here,"

and walks him out to the Brooklyn Ferry honking in the driveway.

*

Walt Whitman, when I opened your book again this morning I thought
      I saw a page slip out from between "A Promise to California,"
      and "A Leaf for Hand in Hand," but it was just the robust love
      of my neglected utility bill.
And yet, the way it fell, first gliding, catching the light from the east
      window, then end over end, it almost made me want to write
      a check for all that I have left unpaid.
Because a body has to pay the bills, and loves to walk to the store
      in winter and buy a newspaper and stamps for later
      and a coffee for now.
Because the soul is always looking around for its likeness in the limbs
      arching over the concrete, or in the specter of the yellow
      bicycle lying in the snow, or in the eyes of the woman
      at the register whose name tag says "Mary Shelley," though she
      does not know the other Mary Shelley, and certainly claims no
      relation, though what body is not a relation?
Which is to say, Walt Whitman, lover of loitering horses, stenographer
      to the stars, that when I write my check for two hundred
      and some odd dollars, and I lick the dry envelope, my tongue
      on the paper will make a sound not unlike a shoe pressing
      into snow.
A body and a soul.
Body licks the envelope.
            Soul walks quietly across the white field

*

and knocks on my door and hands me a pamphlet in which all
the letters are O's.

When I invite my soul in he runs his hand along the walls
to check for hidden mirrors.

He squints his eyes at me as if to tell my fortune: "Weren't you wearing that shirt eight years ago?"

When I ask my soul if he is the alpha or the omega, dream or fact:
"Here's five bucks," he says. "You need a damn haircut"

He sits down, and I bring the tea and biscuits, a remedy for amnesia.
He talks about his life as the moon,

and as the dog for whom the moon is a bone in a distant stew.
He says he does not worry

where he will live after my breath is a bogus address. When I ask
what time his train departs,

he says, "The caboose's future is the engine's past"

*

To speak of the soul is to invite criticism:
 Dear Criticism, your company is requested
at the home of Walt Whitman, cosmic bamboozler,
 revisionist of the grass; you, your lover,
  or husband, or wife, are warmly welcome;
mechanics, southerners, new arrivals, your cousins,
  your complaints, fears, early memories, your lizards,
   your pot-bellied pigs, swearing parakeets,
  that gorilla that speaks sign language (KoKo?)
   your drunk friends, your grudges, your bad checks,
    your motel matchbooks, your anima and animus,
   your spirit coyote, your dream logic and sepia
    tinted photographs, all, all are welcome!

*

I walk over to help my octogenarian neighbor fill the hole
beneath the fence where his dog dug out; he hands me
a shovel and says "I'll put in a wood fence next spring,"
and adds, without a shred of self pity, "if I'm around
that long." Then he shapes his mouth into an O
and widens his eyes and holds his hands up in his best
impersonation of a ghost, a glad ghost, a laughing ghost

with his Labrador running around him in circles.
An old man living in the knowledge of his death,
of the hour approaching when he will leave his house,
and leave his workshop with its wall of ham radios,
and leave all the antennas sprouting like corn
along the edge of his roof, and the frequencies that pull
a million voices through the air.
                              How not to think of you there,
Walt Whitman, spokesmodel for the universe, pamphleteer
of the snowflake and the cloud and the uncombed hair,
all of it an instance of soul – my neighbor and his dog
and the middle of the day and the gravel we shovel
before adding the dirt, and the dirt we tamp down lightly,
and the grass we place on top of that, grass that you loved,
exhibit "A" in the case for life everlasting, great-great-
grandchild of the grass from ages ago, grass which is
its own museum, which grows out of itself, then dies,
then grows again, in the ditch – the Lord's carpet,
by the railroad tracks – the loose cargo's landing strip,
grass in the cracks of the sidewalk, grass which is its own
sidewalk where the living and the dead step toward each other.

James Kimbrell
The Kenyon Review
New Series, Volume XXVII Number 3
Summer 2005

You Got a Song, Man

For Robert Creeley (1926-2005)

You told me the son of Acton's town nurse
would never cross the border
into Concord, where the Revolution
left great houses standing on Main Street.
Yet we crossed into Concord, walking
through Sleepy Hollow Cemetery
to greet Thoreau, his stone
stamped with the word *Henry*
jutting like a gray thumbnail
down the path from Emerson
and his boulder of granite.
We remembered Henry's night in jail,
refusing tax for the Mexican War,
and I could see you hunched with him,
loaning Henry a cigarette, explaining
the perpetual wink of your eye
lost after the windshield
burst in your boyhood face.
When Emerson arrived,
to ask what you and Henry
were doing in there, you would say:
You got a song, man, sing it.
You got a bell, man, ring it.

You hurried off to Henry in his cell
before the trees could bring their flowers
back to Sleepy Hollow.
You sent your last letter months ago
about the poems you could not write,
no words to sing when the president swears
that God breathes the psalms of armies in his ear,
and flags twirl by the millions
to fascinate us like dogs at the dinner table.
You apologized for what you could not say,
as if the words were missing teeth
you searched for with your tongue,

and then a poem flashed across the page,
breaking news of music interrupting news of war:
You got a song, man, sing it.
You got a bell, man, ring it.

Today you died two thousand miles from Sleepy Hollow,
somewhere near the border with Mexico, the territory
Thoreau wandered only in jailhouse sleep.
Your lungs folded their wings in a land of drought
and barbed wire, boxcars swaying like drunks at 3 A.M.
and unexplained lights hovering in the desert.
You said: *There's a lot of places out there, friend,*
so you would go, smuggling a suitcase of words
across every border carved by the heel
of map makers or conquerors, because
you had an all-night conversation with the world,
hearing the beat of unsung poems in every voice,
visiting the haunted rooms in every face.
Drive, you said, because poets must
bring the news to the next town:
You got a song, man, sing it.
You got a bell, man, ring it.

Martín Espada
The Massachusetts Review
Volume 46, Number 3
Fall 2005

Jittery

Nancy takes me to a coffee shop called "Jitters"
which is, I'm thinking, like naming a bar "Drunk":
what you get when you get too much of what it is

they've got to give you – though that's just me
of course, going off. I'm feeling kind of drunk
on talk and too much coffee and Nancy's laughing

easy like she maybe thinks: *okay*. Me, I mean,
though I'm reading into things of course –
talk, laughter – speed-reading into things

what with all the coffee and little sleep
I'm running on of late. Things, their course,
have not been great though I'm feeling not

unhappy to be alive and not asleep and here
with Nancy blabbing out my life like some black
and white Karl Malden movie tough guy grateful

to finally confess and yes I'll obsess on
splitting that infinitive since Nancy knows
syntax ("*syn-*, together + *tassein*, to arrange");

Nancy knows yoga, Neruda, dogs, and *yes*
to the body's thoughtless crush on the world and
her smile flies open like a sun-flushed dove

and right, I know I talk too much and think
too much about what I'm thinking and not
enough about what I say, and simmer too long

in the crock of myself, which is right where I
get when I get this way and want to say
shut up, Simmerman, just shut up. . . .

Nancy takes me to a coffee shop.

Jim Simmerman
American Children
BOA Editions, Ltd.

Counterman

What'll it be?

Roast beef on rye, with tomato and mayo.

Whudduhyuh want on it?

A swipe of mayo.
Pepper but no salt.

You got it. Roast beef on rye
. . . You want lettuce on that?

No. Just tomato and mayo.

Tomato and mayo. You got it.
. . . Salt and pepper?

No salt. Just a little pepper.

You got it. No salt.
You want tomato.

Yes. Tomato. No lettuce.

No lettuce. You got it.
. . . No salt, right?

Right. No salt.

You got it. – Pickle?

No, no pickle. Just tomato and mayo.
And pepper.

Pepper.

Yes, a little pepper.

Right. A little pepper.
No pickle.

Right. No pickle.

You got it.
Next.

Roast beef on whole wheat, please,
With lettuce, mayonnaise and a center slice
Of beefsteak tomato.
The lettuce splayed, if you will,
In a Beaux Arts derivative of classical acanthus,
And the roast beef, thinly sliced, folded
In a multi-foil arrangement
That eschews Bragdonian pretensions
Or any idea of divine geometric projection
For that matter, but simply provides
A setting for the tomato
To form a medallion with a dab
Of mayonnaise as a fleuron.
And – as eclectic as this may sound –
If the mayonnaise can also be applied
Along the crust in a Vitruvian scroll
And as a festoon below the medallion,
That would be swell.

You mean like in the Cathedral St. Pierre in Geneva?

Yes, but the swag more like the one below the rosette
At the Royal Palace in Amsterdam.

You got it.
Next.

Paul Violi
Shiny
Number 13

International Incidents

1.

Wang Ping asks if
we went to a seder
last night
        She did,
in Minneapolis
No, I say, we're not
observant
as though we constantly
overlook details

2.

The teachers in the lounge
crowd around the
Swedish visitor
You must be very proud
one of them beams
to be Swedish
She has no idea
what that means
She says,
I don't *dislike*
being Swedish

3.

Who's ever met a Bulgarian?
he would shout in the bar
Then one night
two homely blond sisters
smiled and said
We are Bulgarians!
They smiled for two weeks
then went away forever

Robert Hershon
Calls from the Outside World
Hanging Loose Press

Some Days I Feel Like Janet Leigh

Some days I feel like Janet Leigh in *Touch of Evil* –
I wake up, sunny and blond, but by the time midnight
rolls around I've been hijacked by Akim Tamiroff's
greasy thugs, shot up with heroin, framed for murder,
and I'm out cold in a border town jail. I didn't kill
Akim, of course, it was Hank Quinlan – drunk, overweight
Orson Welles – who for thirty-odd years as sheriff
has been framing creeps for crimes they maybe did. Enter
Mike Vargas, tall handsome Mexican cop – Charlton
Heston with a weird little mustache and a dark tan
from a can. "You don't talk like a Mexican," Welles
says to Heston, which speaks to me, because talking
like a Mexican could solve any number of roadside hells
I am currently running away from – well, walking.

Barbara Hamby
Five Points
Volume 9, Number 3

Local Heroes

The Feast of All Souls, 2001

Some days the worst that can happen happens.
The sky falls or evil overwhelms or
the world as we have come to know it turns
toward the eventual apocalypse
long predicted in all the holy books –
the end-times of old grudge and grievances
that bring us each to our oblivions.
Still, maybe this is not the end at all,
nor even the beginning of the end.
Rather, one more in a long list of sorrows
to be added to the ones thus far endured,
through what we have come to call our history –
another in that bitter litany
that we will, if we survive it, have survived.
God help us who must live through this, alive
to the terror and open wounds: the heart
torn, shaken faith, the violent, vengeful soul,
the nerve exposed, the broken body so
mingled with its breaking that it's lost forever.
Lord send us, in our peril, local heroes.
Someone to listen, someone to watch, someone
to search and wait and keep the careful count
of the dead and missing, the dead and gone
but not forgotten. Some days all that can be done
is to salvage one sadness from the mass
of sadnesses, to bear one body home,
to lay the dead out among their people,
organize the flowers and casseroles,
write the obits, meet the mourners at the door,
drive the dark procession down through town,

toll the bell, dig the hole, tend the pyre.
It's what we do. The daylong news is dire –
full of true believers and politicos,
bold talk of holy war and photo-ops.
But here, brave men and women pick the pieces up.
They serve the living, caring for the dead.
Here the distant battle is waged in homes.
Like politics, all funerals are local.

Thomas Lynch
Michigan Quarterly Review
Volume XLIV, No. 4
Fall 2005

Black Labrador

1.

Churchill called his bad visits from depression
a big black dog. We have reversed that, Winston.
We've named him Nemo, no one, a black hole
where light is gulped – invisible by night:
by day, when light licks everything to shine,
a black silk coat ablaze with inky shade.
He's our black lab, wherein mad scientists
concoct excessive energy. It snows,
and he bounds out, inebriate of cold.
The white flakes settle on his back and neck and nose
and make a little universe.

2.

It's best to take God backward; even sideways
He is too much to contemplate, "a deep
but dazzling darkness," as Vaughan says.
And so I let my Nemo-omen lead me
onward and on toward that deep dark I'm meant
to enter, entertain, when my time comes . . .
The day wheels past, a creaky cart. I study
the rippling anthracite that steadies me,
the tar, the glossy licorice, the sable;
and in this snowfall that I should detest,
late March and early April, I'm still rapt
to see his coat so constellated, starred, re-starred,
making a comic cosmos I can love.

David Young
Black Lab
Alfred A. Knopf, Publisher

Index of Names and Titles

[I want to build], 90
"*Off in the darkness hourses moved restlessly*", 167
13 Haiku About My Husband and Current State of Happiness, 39-40

A

A Stick, A Cup, A Bowl, A Comb, 70-71
About the Money, 78-79
Absence, 58-59
Acrostic: Outhouse, 53
Allen, Richard D., 155
Anatomy of Failure, 43
And Day Brought Back My Night, 44
Anderson, Daniel, 7-8
Anent the Yellow Field, Fa-La, 41
Animal Self, 33
Ansel, Talvikki, 159
Antin, David, 126-135
Antler, 54
Appalachian Farewell, 182
Aristophanes at the Woodpile, 157
Armitage, Simon, 94
Army Tales, 160-161
Ars Poetica, 191-192
At Home, 55
Aungier, Liam, 91

B

Baker, David, 187-188
Ball, Jesse, 118
Barańczak, Stanisław, 28
Barbarese, J.T., 141-142
Barnstone, Aliki, 86
Bear, The, 101
Big Doors, 184
Black Labrador, 225
Blackbird, 75-76
Blasing, Randy, 33
Blue Umbrella, 150-151

Board Book & the Costume of a Whooping Crane, 72-74
Bogen, Deborah, 125
Bohince, Paula, 53
Brackenbury, Alison, 3
Brock, Geoffrey, 44
Brouwer, Joel, 30
Budy, Andrea Hollander, 209

C

Cahill, Jennifer Fumiko, 113
Campion, Peter, 95
Canaday, John, 100
Cavafy, C.P., 86-87
Cavanaugh, Clare, 28
Chair She Sits In, The, 149
Chandhok, Lynn Aarti, 96
Chang, Jennifer, 60-61
Charles Street, Late November, 164
Chess Match Ends in Fight, 99
Chiasson, Dan, 101
Chitwood, Michael, 42
Chute, Robert, 157
Claus, Hugo, 55
Closson Buck, Paula, 152-153
Concerning a Young Woman, 25
Contract Law, 77
Counterman, 219-220

D

Darkness Starts, 178
Death of a Gull, 10-11
Death, Etc., 180-181
Demise of Camembert, The, 67-68
Dennis, Carl, 88-89
Dent, Tony, 12
Description of a Lost Thing, 106
Dress Rehearsal, 124
Dunn, Stephen, 189-190

E

Edelstein, Carol, 92
Edge, 5
Elder, Karl, 202-205
Elegance, 105
Elena Ceauçescu's Bed, 69
Emerson, Claudia, 26
Empty Similes, 108
Enemies of Enormity, 116-117
Espada, Martín, 215-216
Evening Star, The, 4

F

Faced with 8:38, 137-138
Far Niente, 104
Feeding the Fire, 156
Ferry, David, 21-24
Fire Museum, The, 113
First Breath Last Breath, 54
First Love, 28
Fried, Daisy, 154
Friedman, David Joel, 36
Funkhouser, Erica, 164

G

Galvin, Brendan, 6
Garland, Max, 80-81
Ghazal, 115
Glaser, Elton, 19
Glück, Louise, 4
Goldbarth, Albert, 167, 197-198
González, Kevin A., 185
Gonzalez, Ray, 201
Goodyear, Dana, 27
Greenway, William, 143
Greger, Debora, 109-110
Gregg, Linda, 105
Grennan, Eamon, 5
Groarke, Vona, 37

H

Hacker, Marilyn, 115
Hahn, Susan, 195-196
Hamby, Barbara, 222
Hart, Kevin, 158
Haxton, Brooks, 41
Hephaistos, 91
Hernandez, David, 99
Hershon, Robert, 221
Hicok, Bob, 108
Hirsch, Edward, 2
Hoffman, Daniel, 207
Holderlin, Friedrich, 90
Home Front and Gardens, 19
Honey Suckles, 18
Hoopoe's Crown, The, 47-52
Horseneck Beach Odalisque, 57
House Guest, 114
Huge Fragility, 12
Hummingbird, 13

I

I Followed a Ribbon, 118
Icarus Descending, 92
In a Field, 199
Inez, Colette, 112
Insistence of Beauty, The, 189-190
International Incidents, 221
Irons, John, 55
[I want to build], 90

J

Jennings, Edison, 156
Jernigan, Amanda, 206
Jittery, 217-218
Jones, Rodney, 65-66
Jordan, June, 144-145

K

Kane, Mary, 39-40
Karr, Mary, 102
Kasischke, Laura, 121-122
Keepsake, 165
Kenney, Richard , 162

Kenyon, Jane, 20
Kimbrell, James, 211-214
Kirchwey, Karl, 15-17
Kitty Oppenheimer Tends Louis Slotin after an Accident in the Lab, 100
Klink, Joanna, 9
Koethe, John, 168-177
Komunyakaa, Yusef, 179
Kooser, Ted, 107
Kumin, Maxine, 180-181

L

Lamb by Its Ma, A, 56
Lamon, Laurie, 123
Late Beauty, 15-17
Latents, 29
Lauinger, Ann, 31
Laux , Dorianne, 13
Leight, Peter, 119-120
Lesser Evils, 30
Liu, Timothy, 85
Local Heroes, 223-224
Locust Song, The, 197-198
Logan, William, 57
Logo Rhythms, 202-205
Long Marriage, The, 45
Lullabye, 206
Lux, Thomas, 82
Lynch, Thomas, 223-224

M

Macari, Anne Marie, 58-59
Marriage Must Be Worked At, A, 42
Marvell Noir, 31
Mathis, Cleopatra, 10-11
Mazur, Gail, 150-151
McHugh, Heather, 104
Medical Advice, 34
Merwin, W.S., 186
Miłosz, Czesław, 191-192
Miscegenation, 210
Miss Congeniality, 121-122
Molinary, Mary, 136-138
Monsour, Leslie, 32

My Father's Track and Field Medal, 2
My First Mermaid, 109-110
My Mother's Hands, 62
My Mother's Poem, 194
Mycorrhizae, 159

N

Near Hag's Head, 63
New Year, with Nipperkin, 162
Noah at Dusk, 93
Nothing's As It Should Be, 84

O

Oasis, 27
Oatmeal, 38
Obedience, Or the Lying Tale, 60-61
O'Driscoll, Dennis, 98
"Off in the darkness hourses moved restlessly", 167
Old Age, 207
On Broadway, 85
On us too, 138
One-Time Use, 155
O'Rourke, Meghan, 43
Osherow, Jacqueline, 47-52
Our Generation, 88-89

P

Pain Tries to Think of Something, 123
Pankey, Eric, 111
Peter Street , 64
Phillips, Robert, 84
Pier Aspiring, The, 82
Pity of Punctuation, The, 195-196
Population, The, 95
Postmortem, 208
Prescience, 183
Private Meditations of John Wyclif, The: On Angels, 103
Prufer, Kevin, 160-161

R

Racial Profile #2, 144-145
Rattlesnakes Hammered on the Wall, 201
Rector, Liam, 78-79
Re-Gifting, 37
Report from My Own Backyard, 152-153
Resistance, 119-120
Riffing Deciduous, 6
Ríos, Alberto, 149
Rivard, David, 116-117
Rosser, J. Allyn, 97
Rossini, Clare, 208
Ryan, Kay, 29
Ryan, Michael, 139

S

Sand, 14
Santos, Sherod, 25
Sappho, 25
Satterlee, Thom, 103
Scharf, Michael, 77
Schemes, 3
Schwartz, Hillel, 146-148
Selling Out, 98
Seyburn, Patty, 14
Shapiro, Alan, 46
Sheerin, Joel, 34
Shout, The, 94
Shumaker, Peggy, 38
Simic, Charles, 106
Simmerman, Jim, 217-218
Simpson, Louis, 83
Sirr, Peter, 64
Six at the Beginning, 125
Skeen, Tim, 140
Skinner, Jeffrey, 45
Skloot, Floyd, 124
Slate, Ron, 67-68
Small parts slowly, 136-137
Snodgrass, W.D., 69
Snow, 158
Sobin, Gustaf, 193
Some Days I Feel Like Janet Leigh, 222

Sounding Aboard the Rafaella, 35
Spanish Lover, The, 26
Spires, Elizabeth, 199
Stein, Kevin, 166
Stern, Gerald, 163
Still Life With Jonquils, 209
Stroke, 143
Subway Seethe, 97
Suddenly, 83
Sunflowers in a Field, 7-8
Sursum Corda, 146-148
Sylvia, 163
Szymborska, Wisława, 28

T

Takeoff, 46
talking at blerancourt, 126-135
Teague, Alexandra, 114
Testament, 193
They Had Torn Off My Face at the Office, 107
Tillinghast, Richard, 184
To Failure, 140
To the Soul, 186
To You, 185
Tobin, Daniel, 63
Travel Plans, 32
Tree Ghost, 179
Trethewey, Natasha, 210
Trying to Be Penitent, 141-142
Twichell, Chase, 56
Twilight: After Haying, 20
Two Children Threatened by a Nightingale, 111
Two Wheeler Spins, 112

U

United States, The, 65-66
Unlasting, The, 168-177
Up Late, Reading Whitman, 211-214
Used One Speed, Princeton, 154

V

Very Hot Day, 139
View From Zero Bridge, The, 96
Violi, Paul, 219-220
Virgil, 21-24
Virgil: from the Second Georgic, 21-24

W

Wagoner, David, 194
Welcome, The, 36
When the Watchman Saw the Light,
    86-87
White Heron Pond, 187-188
White, Philip, 165
Who the Meek Are Not, 102
Wier, Darta, 70-71
Wilder, Rex, 35
Williams, C.K., 75-76
Wiman, Christian, 178
Winter Field, 9
Wishful Rhetoric, 166
Witek, Terri, 93
Wojahn, David, 72-74
Wolff, Daniel, 18
Woo, David , 62
Wright, Charles, 182
Wright, Franz, 183

Y

You Got a Song, Man, 215-216
You Miss It, 80-81
Young, David, 225

Permissions

"13 Haiku About My Husband and Current State of Happiness" reprinted from *Beloit Poetry Journal* with the permission of Mary Kane.

"About the Money" from *American Poetry Review*, Copyright © 2005 by World Poetry, Inc. Reprinted with permission of Liam Rector.

"Absence" from GLORYLAND. Copyright © 2005 by Anne Marie Macari. Reprinted with the permission of Alice James Books.

"Acrostic: Outhouse" reprinted from *Beloit Poetry Journal* with the permission of Paula Bohince.

"Anatomy of Failure" first appeared in *The New Republic*. From HALFLIFE by Meghan O'Rourke. Copyright © 2007 by Meghan O'Rourke. Used by permission of W.W. Norton & Company, Inc.

"And Day Brought Back My Night" from WEIGHING LIGHT by Geoffrey Brock. Copyright © 2005 by Geoffrey Brock. Reprinted by permission of the author and Ivan R. Dee, Publisher.

"Anent the Yellow Field, Fa-La" reprinted from *TriQuarterly* with the permission of Brooks Haxton.

"Animal Self" reprinted from *Michigan Quarterly Review* with the permission of Randy Blasing.

"Appalachian Farewell" from SCAR TISSUE by Charles Wright. Copyright © 2006 by Charles Wright. Reprinted by permission of Farrar, Straus and Giroux, LLC. (Printed by Sarabande Books in the chapbook *Wrong End of the Rainbow* in 2005)

"Aristophanes at the Woodpile" reprinted from *Beloit Poetry Journal* with the permission of Robert Chute.

"Army Tales" reprinted from *Colorado Review* with the permission of Kevin Prufer.

"The Evening Star" from AVERNO by Louise Glück. Copyright © 2006 by Louise Glück. Reprinted by permission of Farrar, Straus and Giroux, LLC.

"Far Niente" reprinted from *TriQuarterly* with the permission of Heather McHugh.

"Feeding the Fire" reprinted from *The Kenyon Review* with the permission of Edison Jennings.

"The Fire Museum" reprinted from *Gulf Coast* with the permission of Jennifer Fumiko Cahill.

"First Breath Last Breath" reprinted from *Denver Quarterly* with the permission of Antler.

"First Love" from MONOLOGUE OF A DOG, copyright © by Wislawa Szymborska, 2002, English translation copyright © 2006 by Harcourt, Inc., reprinted by permission of the publisher.

"Ghazal: Waiting" reprinted from the *Virginia Quarterly Review* with the permission of Marilyn Hacker.

"Hephaistos" reprinted from *Poetry Ireland Review* with the permission of Liam Aungier.

"Home Front and Gardens" from HERE AND HEREAFTER. Copyright © 2005 by Elton Glaser. Reprinted with permission of University of Arkansas Press.

"Honey Suckles" reprinted from *Western Humanities Review* with the permission of Daniel Wolff.

"The Hoopoe's Crown" from THE HOOPOE'S CROWN, Copyright © 2005 by Jacqueline Osherow. Reprinted with permission of BOA Editions, Ltd. All rights reserved.

"Horseneck Beach Odalisque", from THE WHISPERING GALLERY by William Logan, copyright © 2005 by William Logan. Used by permission of Penguin, a division of Penguin Group (USA) Inc

"House Guest" reprinted from *Crazyhorse* with the permission of Alexandra Teague.